D1457460

OUR WONDERFUL JUDGE

Abiding in His Love

Allan W. Freed, PhD

TEACH Services, Inc.
P U B L I S H I N G
www.TEACHServices.com • (800) 367-1844

Copyright © 2020 Allan W. Freed
Copyright © 2020 TEACH Services, Inc.
ISBN-13: 978-1-4796-1050-1 (Paperback)
ISBN-13: 978-1-4796-1051-8 (ePub)
Library of Congress Control Number: 2019939100

The Scripture used throughout, unless otherwise noted, is taken from the New King James Version®. Copyright © 1982 by Thomas Nelson. Used by permission. All rights reserved.

Other versions used include the Amplified Bible, Classic Edition (AMPC) copyright © 1954, 1958, 1962, 1964, 1965, 1987 by The Lockman Foundation; the King James Version (KJV); and the NET Bible® copyright ©1996-2006 by Biblical Studies Press, L.L.C. http://netbible.com All rights reserved. The *Common English Bible* (Nashville, TN: Common English Bible, 2011).

Published by

TEACH Services, Inc.
P U B L I S H I N G
www.TEACHServices.com • (800) 367-1844

Dedication

*To my wife Shirley
and to our three children,
Nels, Janine, and Darren*

Finally, there is laid up for me the crown of
righteousness, which the Lord, the righteous Judge,
will give to me on that Day, and not to me only
but also to all who have loved His appearing.
2 Timothy 4:8

*   *   *

And His name shall be called Wonderful, Counselor,
Mighty God, Everlasting Father, Prince of Peace.
Isaiah 9:6

Table of Contents

SECTION TWO
Christ Our Righteousness and Sanctification by Faith

SECTION THREE
Christ Our Righteousness and the Sanctuary

SECTION FOUR
Christ Our Righteousness—Our Wonderful Judge

SECTION FIVE
Christ Our Righteousness in Perilous Times

SECTION SIX
Christ Our Righteousness All Through Eternity

Preface

Some years ago I was at a meeting for Seventh-day Adventist workers. At the close of one presentation, the presenter opened the floor for questions and answers. I read the following quotation and followed it with an observation and a final question.

> Let us seek the Lord with the whole heart, that we may find Him. We have received the light of the three angels' messages; and we now need to come decidedly to the front, and take our position on the side of truth. The fourteenth chapter of Revelation is a chapter of deepest interest. This scripture will soon be understood in all its bearings, and the messages given to John the revelator will be repeated with distinct utterance.[1]

"I can see the second angel's message being repeated," I said, "because it is repeated in Revelation 18:1–4, and the third angel's message will be repeated because it will be given with decided effectiveness in opposition to Sunday legislation. My question is: What about the first angel's message? Will a judgment hour message be repeated when the judgment passes from the dead to the living?"

Since the 1990s, several Adventist publications on the judgment have appeared. In adding this little volume, it is my desire to show how we may cooperate with our Lord and Savior in the final phase of the atonement. The blessing of the final atonement for the living is to have our sins blotted out and to be sealed into oneness with Christ for eternity. The intent

---

[1] *Review and Herald*, Oct. 13, 1904.

of the following pages is to support all believers in their appreciation of this high privilege. Some phrases and concepts are repeated throughout the book. I have used such repetition on purpose so that new readers may become familiar with these phrases and concepts.

I pray that you will consult the many references given so that the concepts will become a part of your Christian walk with Christ. Deep thanks and appreciation go to all who have encouraged me to put my thoughts on this subject into writing. I want to say a special "thank you" to Carol Nicks, Pastor Nathan James, Pastor David Beaudoin, Keith Clouten, Dale Burns, Glen Pearson, and others who contributed their invaluable suggestions and insights. Special thanks are also due my wife, Shirley, for her quiet and thoughtful encouragement along the way.

Introduction

Since my conversion, I have had a keen interest in the way Jesus is preparing us for His soon return. It is apparent that sin disrupted the oneness and communion that humanity had with our loving heavenly Father in the beginning. Seeing the conflict between good and evil, as portrayed in Scripture and through my own experience, caused me to search diligently for my role in this great controversy. The results of my search are this book, by which I share with others my understanding of how God—through Christ our Righteousness—is restoring our unity with Him, especially during the final phase of the atonement—the judgment of the living. The process of making atonement is the process of restoring "at-one-ment" with God. To cooperate with God in restoring this oneness, we need to see who Jesus is and what He is doing for us in the heavenly sanctuary. Therefore, the first part of this book is devoted to who Jesus is.

What I have written is the result of a lifetime of praying, searching the Scriptures, and studying the Spirit of Prophecy to understand God's plan for our salvation. Basic principles in understanding the Bible as well as the writings of Ellen White (see APPENDIX) have guided my search. This short work summarizes my understanding that Christ is indeed our Wonderful Judge. The term "Wonderful Judge" is a combination of concepts from Isaiah 9:6 and Acts 10:42.

Presented in this book is an overview of salvation from the Fall to the Restoration, with emphasis on the person and work of Christ as our Righteousness and Wonderful Judge in the heavenly sanctuary.[2]

SECTION ONE looks at the person of Christ and what He became for us in order that we might be set right, or justified, with our heavenly Father.

---

[2] *Christian Service*, p. 349.

SECTION TWO examines how we live, which is sanctification, as we continue to focus on God's great mercy for us in Christ Jesus.

SECTION THREE is a review of the sanctuary and its imagery as they relate to Christ our Righteousness and the plan of salvation throughout Scripture.

The first three sections lay the foundation for SECTION FOUR, which calls attention to the great hope we have in Christ during the judgment of the living when we are brought into oneness with Christ. It also emphasizes our part in living for Jesus and cooperating with Him in all things.

SECTION FIVE is included as a cautionary message that we not allow ourselves to be deceived in these perilous times by the modern phenomenon in the Christian world that portrays itself as full New Testament Christianity. Certainly this last-day deception aims, if possible, to deceive "even the very elect" (Matt. 24:24). To accomplish this end, it will have to look and act as if it is completely in harmony with original New Testament teachings and portray itself as the dynamic force to unite Christianity.[3] It is under this three-fold union of the "beast," the "dragon," and the "false prophet" (Rev. 16:13–15) that the final application of the atonement in heaven takes place and is described as a thief-in-the-night experience.

SECTION SIX reminds us that, throughout eternity, the redeemed saints never ascribe righteousness or credit to themselves, for all glory, honor, and praise for their salvation belong to Christ our Lord. The eternal song of the redeemed will be the song of Moses and the song of the Lamb.

In this short work, I have not touched on Sunday legislation or other related events that are of interest to Seventh-day Adventists. Also, it is not intended to be a discussion in favor or against any theological debate in current Adventism. My purpose is to discuss our cooperation with Jesus as He concludes His work as our great High Priest in the heavenly sanctuary. It is my prayer that this volume will bless and encourage you in your journey with Christ to His eternal kingdom. As you read about His great love for us, may you be inspired to cooperate with Him fully in the final phase of the Day of Atonement, which prepares us to meet the closing trials of this earth's history.

---

[3] *The Great Controversy*, pp. 588, 589.

CHRIST OUR RIGHTEOUSNESS AND JUSTIFICATION BY FAITH

Chapter 1

Christ—the Second Adam

(As you read through this section and the next, keep in mind that Jesus is also our Wonderful Judge.)

The apostle Paul wrote: "And so it is written, 'The first man Adam became a living being.' The last Adam became a life-giving spirit" (1 Cor. 15:45). In Romans chapter 5, Paul contrasts the offense of Adam with the righteous life of Jesus Christ. Because of Adam's disobedience to God, the consequences of sin have permeated all creation. All creation is suffering from the accumulated effects of sin (Rom. 8:20–23). Christ, as the second Adam, came to bring restoration from the havoc sin has caused and is causing because of Adam's transgression (Acts 3:18–21).

Our sinful condition inherited from the first Adam

In creating, God expressed His love. All was beautiful and perfect. Without question, it was all "very good" (Gen. 1:31).[4] God's intention for Adam and Eve was that they enjoy His creation for eternity. He knew their happiness could be maintained only by their living according to His word. The only thing God required of them was that they believe and obey (Matt. 4:4; Gen. 2:16, 17). This was the kind of requirement a king would make of his subjects—live according to my will for your blessing and good,

---

[4] *Conflict and Courage*, p. 15.

and you will continue to enjoy what I have provided for you. It was not an agreement between equals, although each had a part to play.

It was not a burdensome requirement that God made, for He had created Adam sinless with great powers of intellect and will. Nonetheless, Adam failed to maintain this obedient relationship. It was not hunger that led him to disobey God. Nor was it the size of the misdemeanor that brought about his estrangement from God. It was his disbelieving God's infallible word.

The serpent first enticed Eve to doubt God's word and then to disbelieve. The natural consequence was rebellion against God. Now a rebel, she then became an instrument of Satan to tempt her husband to disobey. Adam chose to disbelieve God's word. He knew what God had said, yet he chose to rebel. He chose the authority of someone else in place of God in his life. As a result, we, as his posterity, are born with a bent to evil—an inclination to disbelieve God, to rebel, and to believe Satan instead (Gen. 3:1–6; Heb. 3:17–19, 4:1, 2). It is important to notice the sequence. First comes doubt, then comes disbelief, then comes rebellion. Eve's fall was not because she believed Satan. It was because she disbelieved God. As Ellen White says, "In the judgment men will not be condemned because they conscientiously believed a lie, but because they did not believe the truth"[5] and "neglected heaven-sent opportunities for learning what is truth."[6]

> "*Eve's fall was not because she believed Satan. It was because she disbelieved God.*"

Doubt, disbelief, and rebellion have been humanity's problem throughout our entire history. At Sinai, the Israelites had an opportunity to respond to God in full belief (see Heb. 4:2). When God spoke His holy law from the mount, the people said, "All that the LORD our God says … we will hear and do it" (Deut. 5:27). God's response was, "Oh, that they

---

[5] *Patriarchs and Prophets*, p. 55.
[6] *The Desire of Ages*, p. 490.

had such a heart in them that they would fear Me and always keep all My commandments" (Deut. 5:29).

It is obvious that, if we doubt what God says, we will inevitably fall into sin. Scripture clearly shows that, as we undertake to live the Christian life without the Holy Spirit's aid, we cannot resist Satan's slightest suggestions to doubt. Indeed, out of our own hearts come temptations to please the fallen desires and intentions of our innate nature (Jer. 17:9; Matt. 15:19; Mark 7:21, 22; Rom. 1:24). Therefore, the only remedy for us, if we are to grow to believe what God says and live in harmony with His principles, is for us to be transformed in our very nature (see John 3:3; 3:5; Rom. 12:2).

The second Adam and the New Covenant

To effect this transformation, Christ came, as the second Adam, to be the head of the human race—One who would grant us a birthright in harmony with God's holy law. The "counsel of peace" between the Father and the Son (Zech. 6:13) resulted in the truth of John 3:16.[7] Christ came to this world to take Adam's place—to be the new representative man for the human race—that through Him all that Adam lost would be regained.[8] Jesus pledged Himself to stand at the head of the human family so that He could adopt our deformed humanity and cover our moral imperfections with the white robe of His righteousness and restore in us the perfection that was lost in Adam (see Rom. 8:29; 1 Cor. 15:49).[9]

To fulfill His promise with the Father, when the fullness of time was come, Jesus came to this world saying, "Behold, I have come—in the volume of the book it is written of Me—to do Your will, O God" (Heb. 10:7).[10] And again He said, "I delight to do Your will, O my God, and Your law is

---

[7] *The Seventh-day Adventist Bible Commentary*, vol. 7, p. 934; *Patriarchs and Prophets*, p. 63.

[8] *Patriarchs and Prophets*, p. 67; see also Christian Support Group Learning Guides, URL, Guide Number 2, "Trouble Gets Its Start."

[9] *The Faith I Live By*, p. 76.

[10] *The Seventh-day Adventist Bible Commentary*, vol. 7, p. 934.

within my heart" (Ps. 40:8). Jesus' obedience to God's holy law is the ful-fillment of His and His Father's pledge. It is the promise of Jesus Himself, as man's representative, to fulfill on our behalf all the conditions of all the covenants that God made with humanity (Gal. 3:27–29; Heb. 8:6).[11]

There are several passages of Scripture that show Jesus to be the sec-ond Adam (1 Cor. 15:45; 15:47; 15:22). Romans 5:11–19 more specifically elaborates on the contrast between Christ and Adam. Verse 14 states: "Nevertheless death reigned from Adam to Moses, even over those who had not sinned according to the likeness of the transgression of Adam, *who is a type of Him who was to come*" (emphasis added).

When Jesus was born into this world, He was called "that Holy One" (Luke 1:35). Never was anything like this said of any of Adam's other descendants, nor could it be. We are born in iniquity, and we go astray from the time of our birth (Ps. 51:5; 58:3; Isa. 48:8). But Jesus is the repre-sentative Man of the human race, the second Adam.[12] He is "holy, harm-less, undefiled, separate from sinners" (Heb. 7:26). There was nothing in Him that would yield to sin—no bent to sin, no tendencies to sin, no evil propensities (Heb. 4:15; 2 Cor. 5:21; John 14:30). He could have sinned just as Adam did. But, He didn't! There was no sin in His being, in His thoughts, or in His actions. He was "without sin" (Heb. 4:15). He was as perfectly sinless as was Adam the moment God created him. He took "His position at the head of humanity by taking the nature but not the sinful-ness of man."[13]

As Adam was the representative man at his creation and fall, so Christ, now the second Adam, is the representative Man for all the human race who accept Him. "Therefore, as through one man's offense judgment came to all men, resulting in condemnation, even so through one Man's righteous act the free gift came to all men, resulting in justification of life" (Rom. 5:18).

---

[11] *The Seventh-day Adventist Bible Commentary*, vol. 7, pp. 931, 933.
[12] *Selected Messages*, book 1, p. 253.
[13] *Signs of the Times*, May 29, 1901.

His humanity means everything to us.[14] When we accept Christ by faith, we are adopted into the heavenly family and participate in the New Covenant experience, which Christ has secured for us (Rom. 8:15; Gal. 4:5–7; Heb. 10:16).[15] Our hearts, emotions, and intentions are changed from disbelief and rebellion into love and the desire to do our heavenly Father's will. The Apostle Paul's prayer for us is: "Now may the God of peace who brought up our Lord Jesus from the dead, that great Shepherd of the sheep, through the blood of the everlasting covenant, make you complete in every good work to do His will, working in you what is well pleasing in His sight, through Jesus Christ, to whom be glory forever and ever. Amen" (Heb. 13:20, 21).

The Father and the Son, in the eternal counsels of heaven, made an everlasting covenant (Zech. 6:13) that, if humanity should sin, Christ would offer His life for their salvation.[16] When on the cross Jesus declared, "It is finished," the everlasting covenant was sealed. Salvation was assured for all. God the Father, through the gospel prophet Isaiah, said

> *"As the second Adam, Christ has restored, in New Covenant relationship with God, all that the first Adam lost."*

of Jesus: "I, the LORD, have called You in righteousness, and will hold Your hand; *I will keep You and give You as a covenant to the people, as a light to the Gentiles*" (Isa. 42:6, emphasis added).[17] Jesus, as the second Adam, became the surety of God's covenant of salvation for both Jew and Gentile. He became our righteousness. He fulfilled the broadest claims of God's holy law (Ps. 119:96) for all who believe (Rom. 10:4). His life

---

[14] *Selected Messages*, book 1, p. 244.

[15] *Selected Messages*, book 1, p. 244.

[16] *Patriarchs and Prophets*, p. 63; *Testimonies for the Church*, vol. 8, p. 269; *Signs of the Times*, May 14, 1902.

[17] See also Isaiah 49:8, 9, and Jeremiah 33:14–16.

stands for the life of us all.[18] He has taken humanity to the highest heavens to sit in heavenly places with Him—that is, in the heavenly sanctuary (Eph. 1:3, 20; 2:6). These texts and Hebrews 9:23 use the same key word—*epouranios*, which means "heavenly." In Hebrews it refers to the heavenly sanctuary.[19] The justifying righteousness we have at the right hand of God brings us "peace with God through our Lord Jesus Christ" (Rom. 5:1). As the second Adam, Christ has restored, in New Covenant relationship with God, all that the first Adam lost.

Man's faulty covenantal relationship redeemed

When God created Adam and Eve, their happy estate could be maintained only by obedience to the heavenly Father (Gen. 2:16, 17).[20] When God made a covenant with Abraham, He said, "Walk before Me and be blameless. And I will make My covenant between Me and you, and will multiply you exceedingly" (Gen. 17:1, 2). The covenant God made with the Israelites was, "Obey and live" (Deut. 5:33; 8:1).[21] History reveals the ups and downs of God's covenant people. Yet, as Solomon prayed, "When they sin against You (for there is no one who does not sin), … and when they return to You with all their heart and with all their soul … then hear in heaven Your dwelling place their prayer and their supplication … and forgive Your people who have sinned against you" (1 Kings 8:46–50). When the Israelites failed in their covenantal relationship with Him, God called them to return, and He graciously forgave them through the blood of the sacrificial animal, which prefigured the blood of Jesus Christ, the "Lamb of God" (Lev. 4:20–35; 5:10–18; Eph. 1:7; John 1:29).

---

[18] *The Desire of Ages*, p. 762.

[19] These are ἐπουράνια (in Heb. 9:23) and ἐπουρανίοις (in Eph. 1:3, 20; 2:6). Both are plural from the root word ἐπουράνιος, signifying "heavenlies" in reference to locality (see *The Analytical Greek Lexicon*, New York, Harper and Brothers, n.d.).

[20] *Conflict and Courage*, p. 15.

[21] *Amazing Grace*, p. 136.

Thus, in the New Covenant, Paul could say, "God demonstrates His own love toward us, in that while we were still sinners, Christ died for us. Much more then, having now been justified by His blood, we shall be saved from wrath through Him. For if when we were enemies we were reconciled to God through the death of His Son, much more, having been reconciled, we shall be saved by His life" (Rom. 5:8–10). When Jesus came to our world, He did for humanity that which humanity could not do for itself (Heb. 10:5–17). He is all that we should be in our New Covenant relationship with God the Father. Only Christ could say, " 'Behold, I have arrived to do Your sovereign will, O God.' He takes away the first [that is, the Old Covenant] in order that He may establish the second [that is, the New Covenant]" (Heb. 10:9, author's translation).

The first covenantal relationship was based on man's obedience (Deut. 5:27–29); the second is based on Christ's obedience as the second Adam to show that man, as God created him, could obey the holy and just law of God.[22] In this He became the "surety of a better covenant" (Heb. 7:22). The apostle says, "But now He has obtained a more excellent ministry, inasmuch as He is also Mediator of a better covenant, which was established on better promises" (Heb. 8:6). The better promises are the promises that Jesus Himself made to fulfill the holy law of God in our behalf. He is "the end [the complete fulfillment] of the law for righteousness to everyone who believes" (Rom. 10:4).[23] "The end," in this instance, means that Christ is the full sum, for righteousness can demand nothing more; it is a complete, holy, undefiled, righteousness that we have in Christ as a free gift imputed to those who are adopted into the family of God. Therefore, by His obedience, He has earned the right to be the mediator of this new and better covenant (Heb. 9:15; 12:24).

We, then, are called out of darkness into the marvelous light of Christ our Savior to be adopted into a new covenantal relationship with Him so

---

[22] *Selected Messages*, book 1, p. 253; *The Seventh-day Adventist Bible Commentary*, vol. 7, p. 912.

[23] "In the new and better covenant, Christ has fulfilled the law for the transgressors of the law, if they receive Him by faith as a personal Saviour" (E. G. White, Letter 276, 1904, July 30, 1904, to David Paulson).

that we may "receive the promise of the eternal inheritance" (Heb. 9:15; cf. 1 Peter 2:9; Rom. 8:15–17). As we receive Christ as Savior, we are justified by faith in His imputed righteousness, which He ministers for us in the heavenly sanctuary. In this justification, we participate in the New Covenant with Christ. The holy law of God is engraved in our hearts by the Spirit of Christ (2 Cor. 3:3). We are transformed into people who love what Christ loves and hate what He hates (Gal. 3:1, 2; Heb. 8:6–10; Rom. 8:1–4). All this is made possible because Christ is the second Adam—the new Father of the human race.

Chapter 2

Christ—Our New Father

In this life, children often lose their parents through war, accident, or sickness. Compassionate people have established orphanages around the world to care for these unfortunate children. Our Redeemer promised He would not leave us as orphans (John 14:18). In receiving Christ as Savior and Lord, we are adopted into the family of God (Rom. 8:15, 16). Through this adoption, we are accepted as sons and daughters of God (Eph. 1:3–6, KJV; Gal. 4:4–6; 1 John 3:2). And, since Christ is the second Adam, He has become, in a special sense, a new spiritual Father for all who will accept Him.

Adopted into the family of God

An Old Testament prophecy refers to Christ as our "Everlasting Father." "And His name will be called Wonderful, Counselor, Mighty God, *Everlasting Father*, Prince of Peace" (Isa. 9:6, emphasis added). One way to understand this is to recognize that He is one with the Father, as He said of Himself in John 10:30. Since this prophecy is about Jesus, another way to understand it is to recognize that, as the Messiah, He is also the Counselor, Mighty God, and everlasting Father of those who accept Him as Savior.[24]

I once heard a parable about a little boy who was playing with the neighbor children, telling his companions how rich his family was.

---

[24] *The Desire of Ages*, p. 483.

Unbeknown to him, his father lost his fortunes through bad decisions. When the little boy learned of it, he could only say to his playmates, "We are poor." In the course of time, his father died, and his mother married a friend of her husband who was also rich. He adopted the little boy as his own. Once again the little boy could say, "We are rich." The question is: What did the little boy do to become rich? He did nothing but to accept his adoption into the family. This simple story illustrates our plight as sinners. Adam, once rich, became poor through a very bad decision. In Adam, we are all poor, lost, and without eternal riches. But, in Christ, we become eternally rich with all that God, in His infinite love and mercy, has to offer (Rom. 8:32). Our wealth is not because of anything we have done but because we are the adopted children of God.

> "*Our wealth is not because of anything we have done but because we are the adopted children of God.*"

Note this insightful remark by Ellen White. "All that man can possibly do toward his own salvation is to accept the invitation, 'Whosoever will, let him take the water of life freely.' Rev. 22:17."[25] From now on we grow in Christ and learn to live as children of the heavenly King (2 Peter 3:18).

Another story, in 2 Samuel 9, illustrates the plight of humanity after the Fall. Mephibosheth, as the only surviving heir of King Saul's dynasty, was in line for the kingship of Israel. In those days, any rival to the throne would be killed. Yet, David searched for Mephibosheth and brought him to his own table to be cared for in the king's house as a son for as long as he should live. Mephibosheth received a new home and a new father, so to speak.

It is easy to see the analogy with humanity. Our first parent, Adam, crippled human nature for all his posterity because of his choice in following his own wisdom instead of depending on God's word. Now we are sinners by birth—rebels and adversaries to the King of the universe. Because

---

[25] *Our High Calling*, p. 122.

of our rebelliousness, we are deserving only of death. But God, in His mercy, gave Adam's posterity a new Father (Isa. 9:6). Not only is Jesus one with the Father, but He is also the everlasting Father of the human race.[26] He has taken humanity upon Himself to be retained for all eternity (John 1:4; 1:14; Phil. 2:5–11).[27] He is the "Son of Man," and He will return to earth the second time as the "Son of Man" (Matt. 8:20; 16:27; Rev. 14:14). Hebrews 10:5 literally reads: "Consequently, entering into the world, He says, 'You did not want sacrifice and offering, but You Yourself united completely to Me a body'" (Heb. 10:5, author's translation).[28] Ellen White insightfully declared that, when "Christ came to this world," He "clothed His divinity with humanity."[29]

Ellen White also wrote: "In taking upon Himself man's nature in its fallen condition, Christ did not in the least participate in its sin."[30] He did not sin in thought, act, or in any aspect of His moral nature. He was sinless in every respect.[31] If this were not so, He could not be our Savior. He Himself would need a savior, and that could never be. In writing about himself, David described all humanity: "Behold, I was brought forth in iniquity, and in sin my mother conceived me" (Ps. 51:5). But of Jesus, the angel said, "That Holy One ["That holy thing," KJV] who is to be born will be called the Son of God" (Luke 1:35).[32] Many other texts describe the complete sinlessness of our Savior, the new Father of the human race.[33]

---

[26] *The Desire of Ages*, p. 483.

[27] *The Seventh-day Adventist Bible Commentary*, vol. 7, pp. 924, 925; *Selected Messages*, book 1, p. 258.

[28] See also *The Seventh-day Adventist Bible Commentary*, vol. 7, p. 1103; and *Questions on Doctrine*, p. 675.

[29] *Christ's Object Lessons*, p. 244.

[30] *Signs of the Times*, June 9, 1898; Ms. 143, 1897.

[31] *Selected Messages*, book 1, p. 256; see also *The Seventh-day Adventist Bible Commentary*, vol. 7, p. 925; also *The Seventh-day Adventist Bible Commentary*, vol. 7, pp. 1126–1131.

[32] *The Desire of Ages*, p. 55; *The Seventh-day Adventist Bible Commentary*, vol. 7, p. 1128.

[33] See 2 Corinthians 5:21; Hebrews 4:15, 2:17–18; John 14:30; and also *The Desire of Ages*, p. 55.

A sinless inheritance through our new Father

Concerning Adam, Ellen White stated that he "was created a pure, sinless being, without a taint of sin upon him; he was in the image of God."[34] Our blessed Lord began "where the first Adam began. Willingly he passed over the ground where Adam fell, and redeemed Adam's failure."[35] He remained as morally pure and spotless in His humanity as Adam was when he came from the creative hand of God.[36] Propensities and tendencies to evil are a result of the Fall.[37] These Jesus did not have. I thank God we have a new Father of the human race—one who is in every way in harmony with our heavenly Father's holy will. In Him we are called to an "inheritance incorruptible and undefiled and that does not fade away, reserved in heaven" for us (1 Peter 1:4).

Our Wonderful Everlasting Father of the human race is the second Adam, the representative Man in whom is fulfilled all the righteousness that is required of us in order to have fellowship with a pure and holy God.[38] Our inheritance of eternal life is secure in Him because "His life stands for the life of men."[39]

---

[34] *The Seventh-day Adventist Bible Commentary*, vol. 7, p. 1128; see also Hebrews 4:15; 7:26.

[35] *Youth's Instructor*, June 2, 1898.

[36] *Questions on Doctrine*, pp. 650, 651; *The Seventh-day Adventist Bible Commentary*, vol. 7, p. 1081.

[37] A "propensity" is an inherent inclination to act in a certain way.

[38] *Selected Messages*, book 1, p. 367.

[39] *The Desire of Ages*, p. 762.

Chapter 3

Christ—Our Substitute

He was wounded for our transgressions,
He was bruised for our iniquities;
The chastisement for our peace was upon Him,
And by His stripes we are healed. (Isa. 53:5)

The dictionary defines "substitute" as "a person or thing" that "takes the place or function of another."[40] Clearly Jesus took our place and did for us what we could not do for ourselves. Over the next few chapters I wish to bring into focus the terms "substitute and surety" and "pattern and example." These are terms that Ellen White frequently used in reference to the redemptive work of our Savior. As our Substitute, Christ loved us and gave Himself for us (Gal. 2:20; Eph. 5:2) "that He might redeem us from every lawless deed and purify for Himself His own special people, zealous for good works" (Titus 2:14).

In the place of my failure

The phrase "substitute and surety" has special and precious meaning when we consider all that it entails. To be our Substitute, Christ had to be what the rest of humanity, after the fall of Adam, was not.[41] Only a person without sin could stand in our place and make us acceptable to a holy

---

[40] *Merriam-Webster Dictionary*, iPad version (accessed 5/31/18).
[41] *Selected Messages*, book 1, p. 256.

God—a God whose eyes are too pure to behold evil (Eph. 1:6, KJV; Hab. 1:13). As we grow in our study of what Christ means to us, we become aware of many allusions in the Bible and the Spirit of Prophecy to Christ's being our Substitute. For instance, as the high priest of ancient Israel was to "bear the iniquity of the congregation" (Lev. 10:17, KJV, NET, etc.), so also did Christ bear our sins on the cross (1 Peter 2:24; 2 Cor. 5:21).

The prophecy of Isaiah 53:4–6 foretold the substitutionary work of our Savior. "Surely He has born our griefs and carried our sorrows; … All we like sheep have gone astray; we have turned, every one, to his own way; and the LORD has laid on Him the iniquity of us all." As our Substitute, He paid the penalty for our transgressions. "By His knowledge," gained through experience, "My righteous Servant shall justify many, for He shall bear their iniquities (Isa. 53:11)." Paul affirmed the same in Romans 5:6: "For when we were still without strength, in due time Christ died for [that is, in the place of] the ungodly." And again, he wrote: "But God demonstrates His own love toward us, in that while we were still sinners, Christ died for us" (Rom. 5:8). Ellen White insightfully declared, "We are not to be anxious about what Christ and God think of us, but about what God thinks of Christ, our Substitute. Ye are accepted in the Beloved. The Lord shows, to the repenting, believing one, that Christ accepts the surrender of the soul, to be molded and fashioned after His own likeness."[42]

Christ not only died the death we deserve, but He also lived the life we are indebted to live. "For if when we were enemies we were reconciled to God through the death of His Son, much more, having been reconciled, we shall be saved by His life (Rom. 5:10)." It is through faith in Christ's substitutionary work for us that the law of Ten Commandments is forever established (Rom. 3:31). He came to earth to fulfill the righteousness of the holy law of God—not only as our Substitute but also as our Surety (Heb. 10:7–9; Ps. 40:8).[43] His righteousness is as limitless as the law of

---

[42] *Selected Messages*, vol. 2, p. 32.

[43] See also *Steps to Christ*, pp. 62, 63; *Selected Messages*, book 1, p. 270; and *The Desire of Ages*, p. 762.

God is holy (Ps. 119:96).[44] It is because of His holy living and holy dying that the New Covenant can now be fulfilled in all who accept Him by faith as their Substitute. He will never fail to redeem us as long as we, with full assurance (Heb. 10:22), live in a saving faith relationship with Him. Saving faith is faith that works by love and purifies the soul (Gal. 5:6). Ellen White further expanded on saving faith when she wrote, "Where there is not only a belief in God's word, but a submission of the will to Him; where the heart is yielded to Him, the affections fixed upon Him, there is faith—faith that works by love and purifies the soul."[45] And so it is that "we must center our hopes of heaven upon Christ alone, because He is our substitute and surety."[46]

Accepted in the Beloved

Job cried in anguish as he sat on the ash heap, "But how can a man be righteous before God?" (Job 9:2). Indeed, how can a sinful person be accepted in the sight of a holy God when He is "of purer eyes than to behold evil, and cannot look on wickedness" (Hab. 1:13). Our greatest need as sinners is to be accepted by our Creator, a holy and righteous God. When we are accepted of Him, He treats us as though we were completely and wholly righteous.[47] This is "to the praise of the glory of His grace, by which He made us accepted in the Beloved" (Eph. 1:6, KJV). It is His grace in Christ Jesus, which He has freely given us, that makes us acceptable in God's sight. Using sanctuary metaphors, Ellen White wrote: "The religious services, the prayers, the praise, the penitent confession of sin ascend from *true believers* as incense to the heavenly sanctuary, but passing through the corrupt channels of humanity, they are so defiled that unless purified by blood, they can never be of value with God. *They ascend*

---

[44] See also the *Common English* and *Amplified Bibles*.

[45] *Steps to Christ*, p. 63.

[46] *Selected Messages*, vol. 1, p. 363.

[47] *Selected Messages*, vol. 1, p. 367.

not in spotless purity, and unless the Intercessor, who is at God's right hand, presents and purifies all by His righteousness, it is not acceptable to God."[48]

It is only through the righteousness of our blessed Lord that true believers approach our heavenly Father. We are encouraged to come "boldly to the throne of grace, that we may obtain mercy and find grace to help in time of need" (Heb. 4:16). When we come to the Father through Jesus our merciful High Priest, we will never be turned away—no matter how sinful we feel or how sinful we see ourselves to be. Jesus said, "The one who comes to Me I will by no means cast out" (John 6:37).

Although we are broken human beings, God has given us a special invitation to come to Him in the name of Jesus. The Apostle Paul says,

> "*When we come to the Father through Jesus our merciful High Priest, we will never be turned away—no matter how sinful we feel or how sinful we see ourselves to be.*"

"Seeing then that we have a great High Priest who has passed through the heavens, Jesus the Son of God, let us hold fast our confession. For we do not have a High Priest who cannot sympathize with our weaknesses, but was in all points tempted as we are, yet without sin. Let us therefore come boldly to the throne of grace, that we may obtain mercy and find grace to help in time of need" (Heb. 4:14–16). We can rejoice in His gracious invitation. Commenting on this scripture, Ellen White also comforts us in the following words, "We come unto God in the name of Jesus by special invitation, and he welcomes us to his audience chamber, and imparts to the humble and contrite heart that faith in Christ by which he is justified, and Jesus blots out as a thick cloud his transgressions."[49]

---

[48] *Selected Messages*, vol. 1, p. 344, emphasis added.
[49] *Christian Education*, p. 128.

Chapter 4

Christ—Our Surety

As we have seen, Jesus is the second Adam, the new Father of the human race, the representative Man, demonstrating that man, as God created him, could obey all of God's commandments from a heart of faith, love, devotion, and adoration.[50] For this reason, He is our Substitute in the New Covenant, which is established on "better promises": the promise that He Himself has fulfilled the broadest claims of God's holy law for us. However, He is not only our Substitute, but He is also our "Surety" in the new and better covenant (Heb. 7:22).

What "surety" means

An incident in my life a number of years ago helped me to understand what "surety" means. Shortly after becoming a Christian, I was working for a construction company that had a bunkhouse where I shared a room with another man. When the guy got to know me, he wanted me to co-sign a loan for him at the bank. In my inexperience, I told him I thought I could do that. We went to the bank together, and the banker asked me if I knew what I was signing. I asked him to explain. He told me I would become *surety* for the loan if the man would default. Not knowing exactly what "surety" meant, I asked him again to explain. He said I would be responsible for the entire amount of money if the man didn't repay the loan. It didn't take me long to realize I could not be surety for a man

---

[50] *Selected Messages*, vol. 1, p. 253; *The Seventh-day Adventist Bible Commentary*, vol. 7, p. 912.

I scarcely knew. I now know that surety means (1) "security against loss or damage, or for the payment of a debt or fulfillment of an obligation," or (2) "a person legally responsible for the debts of another."[51]

Under the New Covenant, Christ has become surety for us. We continuously fall short of God's holy commandments (Rom. 3:23; Gal. 3:22; Rom. 7:12, 14). But, as our Substitute and Surety, Christ has fulfilled the law for us by His perfect obedience. He is the sum of all righteousness that makes us acceptable to God. He became "surety for man to satisfy by His righteousness in man's behalf, the demands of the law."[52] When I first learned this blessed truth, it made my heart sing. I discovered that I have a Savior who has conquered the flesh, the world, and the devil, who is my security, and who can claim all the riches of heaven on my behalf. He is One who can bring me fellowship with the infinite holiness of God! What a wonderful Savior!

Justification by faith in Christ's righteousness

Now, let me share a few words about righteousness by faith. My first introduction to the subject came three years after I was converted. I happened upon the little book *Christ Our Righteousness* by A. G. Daniels. I was thrilled when I read it, and I asked my Bible teacher why I hadn't heard of this before. His said that, since the topic is so difficult to understand, nobody talks about it much. That was then. Today it is not such a foreign subject, but I still hear confused ideas about what righteousness by faith really is. And, I suppose it is no wonder, considering the following statement about the truth of justification by faith, written by Ellen White: "The enemy of man and God is not willing that this truth should be clearly presented; for he knows that if the people receive it fully, his power will be broken. If he can control minds so that doubt and unbelief and darkness

---

[51] *Random House Kernerman Webster's College Dictionary* (2005, 1997, 1991).

[52] *Selected Messages*, vol. 1, p. 257; see also *The Seventh-day Adventist Bible Commentary*, vol. 7, p. 931, and *Selected Messages*, vol. 1, p. 396.

shall compose the experience of those who claim to be the children of God, he can overcome them with temptation."[53] I encourage you to read A. G. Daniells' little book and every other bit of material you can find on this topic.

Here is another statement that inspires my soul. It was written two years after the presentation in 1888 on the message of "Christ our Righteousness."

"The danger has been presented to me again and again of entertaining, as a people, false ideas of justification by faith. I have been shown for years that Satan would work in a special manner to *confuse* the mind on this point.... The point which has been urged upon my mind for years is the *imputed* righteousness of Christ. I have wondered that this matter was not made the subject of discourses in our churches throughout the land, when that matter has been kept so constantly urged upon me … There is not a point that needs to be dwelt upon more earnestly, repeated more frequently, or established more firmly in the minds of all than the impossibility of fallen man meriting anything by his own best works. Salvation is through faith in Christ alone."[54]

Imputed righteousness is of faith

There are two types of righteousness brought to view in Paul's writings, and these are not to be confused. The first is the "righteousness which is of faith" (Rom. 9:30 KJV). This is Christ's righteousness for us in the heavenly sanctuary. It is of faith because "faith is the substance of things hoped for, the evidence of things not seen" (Heb. 11:1). We have it by faith alone imputed to us "apart from works" (Rom. 4:6). The second is the "righteousness of the law … [which is] fulfilled in us who do not walk according to the flesh but according to the Spirit" (Rom. 8:3, 4, see KJV).

---

[53] *Review and Herald*, Sept. 3, 1889, quoted in *Christ Our Righteousness*, (1941), p. 54.
[54] Ellen G. White, Ms. 36, 1890 emphasis added.

The righteousness which is of faith then is not seen. It is reserved in heaven for us where moth cannot eat nor rust corrupt (Matt. 6:20; 1 Peter 1:3–5). We have this righteousness imputed, reckoned, and accounted to us through faith. It is the righteousness of Christ in which there is no shadow of turning (James 1:17). It is the same yesterday, today, and forever (Heb. 13:8). It is a righteousness that fully satisfies the broadest claims of God's holy law (Ps. 119:96; Rom. 10:4).[55] It is the righteousness that justifies us and makes us accepted in the Beloved (Eph. 1:6, KJV; Rom. 5:1, 2). It is New Covenant righteousness (Heb. 10:7, 9). Let this righteousness become the theme and song of your life. Live by it and die by it. It is your only hope. Again, listen to Ellen White's encouraging words to the repentant, believing sinner.

"Righteousness is obedience to the law. The law demands righteousness, and this the sinner owes to the law; but he is incapable of rendering it. The only way in which he can attain to righteousness is through faith. By faith he can bring to God the merits of Christ, and the Lord places the obedience of His Son to the sinner's account.[56] Christ's righteousness is accepted in place of man's failure, and God receives, pardons, justifies, the repentant, believing soul, treats him as though he were righteous, and loves him as He loves His Son. This is how faith is accounted righteousness."[57] Im*put*ed righteousness is *put* to our account in heaven. Im*part*ed righteousness becomes a *part* of us through the Holy Spirit in us.

Imparted righteousness is of the law written in our hearts

On the other hand, the righteousness of the law in our life, through the work of the Holy Spirit in us, is our response in cooperating with Christ

---

[55] *The Great Controversy*, p. 489.

[56] Wherever I see Ellen White's use of the term "merits of Christ," I understand it to mean His substitutionary righteous life and death on my behalf and His intercession for me in the heavenly sanctuary (Rom. 8:34).

[57] *Selected Messages*, book 1, p. 367. Meade MacGuire and M. L. Andreason published their monumental works on victory in Christ before the manuscript releases were published in *Selected Messages*, book 1, in 1958. In part, this accounts for their emphasis on the inward work of grace as righteousness by faith.

for all that He has done for us. When Christ has given His all for us, how can we do anything less than give Him our all? How can we say that, if Christ has done it all, we can live as we please or that it doesn't matter how we live? It is the epitome of selfishness to say, "If my works don't count toward my salvation, then I will do nothing for God and live as I please!" May it never be! With Paul, we will say, I am a slave, a bondservant, to Christ (Rom. 1:1). It is faith in Christ's righteousness ministered in our behalf in the heavenly sanctuary that brings the Holy Spirit into our lives (Gal. 3:1–5). Describing how the new birth comes through the Holy Spirit's work of grace in the believer, Jesus pointed out that this birth from above comes as the result of looking to Christ as the children of Israel looked to the brass serpent that was lifted up in the desert at the time of Moses (John 3:14, 15). As we receive Christ, the Holy Spirit writes the law of God in our hearts (2 Cor. 3:3; Heb. 8:10) and enables us to live the Christian life.

With His law now written in our hearts, we seek to overcome the works of the flesh by looking in faith to Christ our righteousness in the heavenly sanctuary. "For whatever is born of God overcomes the world. And this is the victory that has overcome the world—our faith" (1 John 5:4). We place our faith in Christ's righteousness for us in the heavenly sanctuary because, as it is written, "righteousness without a blemish can be obtained only through the imputed righteousness of Christ."[58] Then, "when we are clothed with the righteousness of Christ, we shall have no relish for sin; for Christ will be working with us. We may make mistakes, but we will hate the sin that caused the sufferings of the Son of God."[59] Our good works in living for Christ are to "proclaim the praises of Him who called" us "out of darkness into His marvelous light" (1 Peter 2:9; cf. 2 Cor. 3:3; Heb. 10:16; 1 John 2:15–17). "For by grace you have been saved through faith, and that not of yourselves; it is the gift of God, not of works, lest anyone should boast. For we are His workmanship, created in Christ Jesus

---

[58] *Review and Herald*, Sept. 3, 1901.
[59] *Review and Herald*, March 18, 1890.

for good works, which God prepared beforehand that we should walk in them" (Eph. 2:8–10).

The righteousness which God works in us by the presence and power of the Holy Spirit is the imparted righteousness of Christ, and it is *imparted* righteousness that becomes a part of us so long as we remain "in Christ" (Col. 1:27, 28). Yet, this righteousness is never to be confused with His *imputed* righteousness, which covers us before the righteous demands of God's holy law in the heavenly sanctuary.[60] Imparted righteousness is the righteousness by which we are sanctified—that is, set apart continuously to live for our Lord Jesus Christ.[61] In this righteousness, we "grow in the grace and knowledge of our Lord and Savior Jesus Christ" (2 Peter 3:18).[62] John Calvin used the sun as an illustration of the different aspects of righteousness. As the sun gives both heat and light, so Christ gives both imputed and imparted righteousness.[63] Just as we would not confuse or substitute the light of the sun for its heat, so we must not confuse the imputed righteousness of Christ, which justifies us, for the imparted righteousness of Christ, which sanctifies us.

> **"Just as we would not confuse or substitute the light of the sun for its heat, so we must not confuse the imputed righteousness of Christ, which justifies us, for the imparted righteousness of Christ, which sanctifies us."**

---

[60] *Steps to Christ*, p. 62.

[61] *Child Guidance*, p. 162; *Christ's Object Lessons*, p. 65.

[62] See also Clifford Goldstein, "Beyond Logic," *Adventist Review*, Jan. 23, 2003, p. 28.

[63] John Calvin, "Of Justification by Faith," *The Institutes of The Christian Religion*, Beveridge edition (1863), Book 3:11.

A Summary of "Christ Our Righteousness"

Christ is holy and righteous. He lived a sinless life, and died in our stead.

(1) Christ *imputes* His righteousness to us.

Christ covers us with His righteousness to satisfy the righteous demands of God's holy law in the heavenly sanctuary. This is the righteousness of faith (Rom. 9:30; 8:34; Isa. 53:12; Heb. 4:14; 8:1).

We accept the redemption in Christ by faith and stand before our holy God justified. (Rom. 3:24–28; 4:6–7).

(2) Christ *imparts* His righteousness to us.

Christ puts His righteousness in our hearts through the Holy Spirit (2 Cor. 3:3) so that we may grow in grace. This is the "**righteousness of the law**" (Rom. 8:4).

We respond in cooperation with Christ's work of sanctification in our lives (Rom. 6:1, 2, 12–15; 3:31).

SECTION TWO

CHRIST OUR RIGHTEOUSNESS AND SANCTIFICATION BY FAITH

Chapter 5

Born into His Family

"Can two walk together, unless they are agreed?" (Amos 3:3)

Jesus prayed that we may be one with Him and be with Him in glory (John 17:24). God's compassionate grace for us is to bring us back so completely into oneness with Him that we will be able to dwell with Him for eternity. During the blessing of the final phase of the atonement (which brings about this oneness), our sins are to be blotted out and we are sealed to live in harmony with our Savior.[64] God brings us to this point as we grow in grace by cooperating with Him in all things.

Some call our growth in the grace of our Lord Jesus Christ *sanctification*. Others view it as *character development*. Whatever we call it, we know that there is a wonderful transformation in our lives when we accept Christ as Savior and abide in Him. Our growth in grace will culminate in reflecting the image of Jesus fully before we enter into His eternal kingdom.[65] God has ordained that we be "conformed to the image of His son" (Rom. 8:29). Scripture and the Spirit of Prophecy tutor us on how to cooperate with Jesus so that we can grow to be like Him. It is imperative that we compare passage with passage when searching the writings of Ellen White on this subject. As we search her writings for all there is on any given topic and read her remarks in context, we will be saved from becoming spiritually lopsided.

---

[64] *Christian Experience and Teachings of Ellen G. White*, p. 105.

[65] We need to remember the parable of the growing seed in Mark 4:26–29. The plant is perfect at every stage. When the full grain is in the ear, the image of the seed is perfectly reproduced. In fact, we do not reflect the image of Jesus *fully* until under the sixth plague. (See *The Great Controversy*, p. 621; *Christ's Object Lessons*, p. 69; and *Early Writings,* p. 71.)

The necessity of the new birth

We should begin this topic with a word about the new birth experience and our cooperation with Jesus in living in the Spirit with Him. It is essential to understand that we experience the new birth by looking to Jesus and accepting what He has done for us, as described in the previous chapters. Jesus said, "And as Moses lifted up the serpent in the wilderness, even so must the Son of Man be lifted up, that whoever believes in Him should not perish but have eternal life" (John 3:14, 15). Accepting Jesus' holy life and death for us is the only way to experience the new birth. Paul shows us the necessity of beholding Jesus as our Savior in order to receive the Holy Spirit. After preaching what he described in First Corinthians as "Christ and Him crucified" (1 Cor. 2:2), Paul asked, "Did you receive the Spirit by the works of the law, or by the hearing of faith?" (Gal. 3:1–3). The obvious answer is that we receive the Holy Spirit by faith in what Christ has done for us.

The way we look to Christ and Him crucified is through His holy Word (Rom. 10:17). The Word and the Spirit are in harmony (John 6:63). We receive the Spirit as we believe the Word of God, which lifts up Christ as our Lord and Savior. The Spirit is "given as a regenerating agent.... Sin could be resisted and overcome only through the mighty agency of the Third Person of the Godhead ... It is by the Spirit that the heart is made pure. Through the Spirit the believer becomes a partaker of the divine nature. Christ has given His Spirit as a divine power to overcome all hereditary and cultivated tendencies to evil, and to impress His own character upon His church."[66] It is only a character which is righteous and faultless that we will take to heaven.[67] And such a character we receive from Christ by faith.

Jesus said we are to live by every word that comes from God. Whether Scripture, Spirit of Prophecy, or God's truth as proclaimed from the pulpit, it is through the Word that Christ is lifted up. By beholding Christ

---

[66] *The Desire of Ages*, p. 671.
[67] *Christ's Object Lessons*, p. 332.

in the Word through faith, we experience the new birth. The Apostle Peter, in speaking of the new birth, used a word with a tense that is difficult to translate into English (see 1 Peter 1:23).[68] It means both "having been born again (NKJV)" and "being born again (KJV)." In harmony with Paul's teaching, Peter says this new birth is brought about through the "word of God which lives and abides forever" (1 Peter 1:23). He affirms that the new birth is not a one-time thing. This is why, in several places, Ellen White talks about being converted daily. Daily conversion means responding to God's word every day as we grow in the grace and knowledge of His holy will (2 Peter 3:18).[69] This daily conversion to God's will is the experience we all must have to conquer sinful tendencies in our lives (1 John 5:4, 5; 2:15–17). By the indwelling of His Holy Spirit, the converting power of God can and will transform our inherited and cultivated tendencies to evil if we surrender our lives unreservedly to Him. The experience of the new birth is demonstrated by a changed life (John 3:3–6; 2 Cor. 5:17).[70] To try to understand or live the Christian life without experiencing the new birth is to attempt an impossibility (1 Cor. 2:14).[71]

> "To try to understand or live the Christian life without experiencing the new birth is to attempt an impossibility."

Nonetheless, each individual's experience may be different. The new birth may be dramatic or it may be imperceptible. Long before the person realizes the presence of God in his or her life, the Holy Spirit is prompting to moral improvement.[72] But it is the new birth through the Word and the Spirit that implants in us a new nature—a spiritual nature (John 3:3–8;

---

[68] The Greek word is ἀναγεγεννημένοι.

[69] The Seventh-day Adventist Bible Commentary, vol. 6, p. 1055; Loma Linda Messages, p. 465; Ms. 8b, 1891.

[70] The Adventist Home, p. 206.

[71] Steps to Christ, p. 59; The Desire of Ages, p. 172.

[72] Steps to Christ, pp. 57, 26.

6:63; 1 Peter 1:23; 2:9; 2 Peter 1:3, 4). Then we grow more and more to live in harmony with His holy will as we cooperate with the Holy Spirit's guidance in our lives (Gal. 5:22–25).

The law of God, written in our hearts by the Holy Spirit through the new birth (Heb. 8:10; 2 Cor. 3:3, 17), is the only true standard of moral living (Rom. 8:3, 4).[73] It is vitally important that we recognize that the law of God is to be written in the entire soul of the person, that is, in the mind, emotions, and the very intentions and desires of the heart. Anything short of this is a deception. Yet, with an unreserved surrender to Christ and the full acceptance of His Holy Spirit working in our lives, there will be love, peace, and delight in having His holy law written in our hearts.[74] God's holy law of Ten Commandments, which are a transcript of His character, is a law of love. It shows us how love behaves itself (Rom. 13:8–10). Therefore, when the law of love is written in our hearts, we will love as Christ loved—with supreme love to God and with love for our neighbor as ourselves (Mark 12:29–31).

What the new birth looks like

Ellen White had much to say about character development. As previously mentioned, character development and sanctification are essentially the same thing. However, before I turn to her writings which emphasize character development, I want to share the Apostle John's concept of sin and salvation. Unless we know what sin is and how to cooperate with Jesus in dealing with it in our lives, we will be struggling and very unhappy Christians. This section requires thoughtful reflection and meditation to understand the concepts presented. Once you understand it, cooperating with Jesus will be the joy of your life.

John says, "Whoever has been born of God does not sin, for His seed remains in him; and he cannot sin, because he is born of God" (1 John 3:9).

---

[73] *Christ's Object Lessons*, p. 315; *Selected Messages*, book 1, p. 317; *The Great Controversy*, p. 7.

[74] Psalm 119:77, 92, 165, 174; 40:8; 2 Thessalonians 2:10, 11, 12; Matthew 5:43–46.

When I first read this passage, I thought, *Wow! That is not my experience.* I began to doubt if I had indeed been born again. As I searched deeper into the meaning of this verse, I found that John is saying: *Those who are born of God cannot continuously go on living in sin.* The new birth has given them a new nature and has implanted the seed of the word of God in their hearts through the Holy Spirit. Consequently, they cannot go on crucifying "again for themselves the Son of God" (Heb. 6:6) by sinning against Him. The diagram below is what I found to be John's doctrine of sin revealed in 1 John 3:9 and 2:1–2, as it relates to our spiritual and sinful natures. Note, in the diagram, the items designated by boldfaced numbers. There are seven in all.

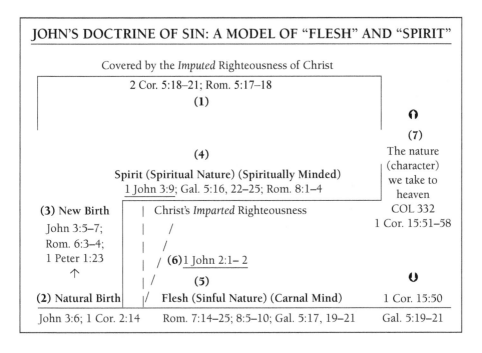

JOHN'S DOCTRINE OF SIN: A MODEL OF "FLESH" AND "SPIRIT"

Covered by the *Imputed* Righteousness of Christ

2 Cor. 5:18–21; Rom. 5:17–18

(1)

(7)
The nature (character) we take to heaven
COL 332
1 Cor. 15:51–58

(4)
Spirit (Spiritual Nature) (Spiritually Minded)
1 John 3:9; Gal. 5:16, 22–25; Rom. 8:1–4

(3) New Birth
John 3:5–7;
Rom. 6:3–4;
1 Peter 1:23

Christ's *Imparted* Righteousness

(6) 1 John 2:1–2
(5)

(2) Natural Birth   Flesh (Sinful Nature) (Carnal Mind)

John 3:6; 1 Cor. 2:14   Rom. 7:14–25; 8:5–10; Gal. 5:17, 19–21   Gal. 5:19–21

We must notice first that Christ's imputed righteousness envelops the world[(1)], for "God was in Christ reconciling the world to Himself, not imputing their trespasses to them" (2 Cor. 5:19; see also Rom. 5:17, 18; 1 John 2:2).[75] This righteousness, however, becomes effectual for us

---

[75] *Steps to Christ*, p. 68.

individually only when we accept Christ as our personal Savior (1 Tim. 4:10). For this reason, the Holy Spirit works with the hearts of all people to bring us to Christ (John 16:8; Jer. 31:3; John 1:9).

The bottom line in the diagram indicates the course of a person's life without Christ. What is born of flesh is of the human natural birth[2] with all its traits, propensities, and tendencies to evil.[76] When we accept Christ as Savior, we experience a new birth[3]. In his Gospel, John wrote, "As many as received Him, to them He gave the right to become children of God, to those who believe in His name: who were born, not of blood, nor of the will of the flesh, nor of the will of man, but of God" (John 1:12, 13). Indeed, in the New Testament, Jesus was the first to contrast the concepts of "flesh" and "spirit" (John 3:6).

Through the new birth, a new spiritual nature is implanted in the heart of the believer[4].[77] In this new nature, believers live in the Spirit with Christ. Then, living in the new spiritual nature with Christ[4], a person cannot go on sinning, that is, living in the sinful nature[5]. We cannot serve two masters at the same time (Matt. 6:24). Romans chapters 7 and 8, and Galatians 5 clearly portray the war between the old sinful nature[5] and the new spiritual nature[4] (see also 2 Cor. 5:17).

But, because of hereditary and cultivated tendencies to sin which remain, the believer does, at times, stumble and fall, as described in the second part of John's doctrine of sin, 1 John 2:1, 2. "My little children, these things I write to you, so that you may not sin [that is, fall into a one-act sin[6]]. And if anybody sins [that is, succumbs to the depravity of the sinful nature], we have an Advocate with the Father, Jesus Christ the righteous. And He Himself is the propitiation for our sins, and not for ours only but also for the whole world." Note the sanctuary imagery of

---

[76] In Scripture, flesh as opposed to spirit carries the Hebrew thought of human as opposed to the Divine, not the Greek thought of body as opposed to soul. In the New Testament flesh is also referred to as "kingdom of darkness," "love of the world." The "flesh" may also mean the character we have apart from Christ (Rom. 7:18).

[77] *Steps to Christ*, pp. 58, 43, 18.

this text. "Propitiation" means "atoning sacrifice," that is, the sacrificial blood applied to the mercy seat of the ark of the covenant.

To summarize the diagram, John's doctrine of sin is the contrast and comparison of 1 John 3:9, "Whoever has been born of God does not sin, for His seed remains in him; and he cannot sin, because he has been born of God," with 1 John 2:1, "My little children, these things I write to you, so that you may not sin. And if anyone sins, we have an Advocate with the Father, Jesus Christ the righteous." It is a contrast between continuously living in the Spirit with Christ[(4)] and falling into a one-act sin[(6)], repenting, and returning to walk in the Spirit with Christ again[(4).] Even though we sin, John assures us that we have Jesus as our Advocate in the heavenly sanctuary to present His blood for the forgiveness of our sins (1 John 2:1, 2). Indeed, it is when we neglect our walk with Christ in the spiritual nature[(4)] that we actually fall into sin[(6)]. It is sin that separates us from God (Isa. 59:2). That is why sin is such a horribly terrible thing.

> "*It cannot be emphasized too strongly that the new birth experience changes our emotional attachments and our way of thinking.*"

When it comes to recognizing sin in our lives, a sensitive conscience may bring upon itself a load of guilt that is not from God. Certainly Satan is the accuser who tries to make us feel that our case is hopeless. It is only through the Holy Spirit that we can come to understand our true condition. Using providence and circumstances, Scripture, reason, and conscience, the Holy Spirit convinces us of sin and leads us to Christ as Savior. Regarding the born-again Christian, Ellen White declared, "A change will be seen in the character, the habits, the pursuits. The contrast will be clear and decided between what they have been and what they are. The character is revealed, not by occasional good deeds[(4)] and occasional misdeeds[(6)], but by the tendency of the habitual words and acts."[78] So my counsel to you

---

[78] *Steps to Christ*, p. 57.

is: don't let Satan beat you up by focusing on the sinfulness of your life. Come to Christ instead and continuously accept His righteousness covering you from the heavenly sanctuary.

It cannot be emphasized too strongly that the new birth experience changes our emotional attachments and our way of thinking. Paul wrote: "But the fruit of the Spirit is love, joy, peace, longsuffering, kindness, goodness, faithfulness, gentleness, self-control. Against such there is no law. And those who are Christ's have crucified the flesh with its passions and desires[5]. If we live in the Spirit, let us also walk in the Spirit"[4] (Gal. 5:22–25). It is evident then that what we used to love before conversion we now hate and vice versa.[79] What our emotions are attached to is what we will tend to do (John 14:15; 15:1–11, NIV). If our emotions are still attached to the things of the world, the battle will go hard between the flesh and the Spirit (Gal. 5:16, 17; 1 Peter 2:11). On the other hand, if we die to self and live for Christ, with our emotions attached to Him, we will live His life (2 Cor. 3:18; Gal. 2:20).[80] Here then is the contrast between setting our affections on the spiritual life in Christ Jesus or cherishing "inordinate affection" (KJV) for the things of the world (Col. 3:1–17; 1 John 2:15–17). The sanctification that brings character development is really a focus of heart love, and, as Pastor Randy Roberts of the Loma Linda University Seventh-day Adventist church once said, "Focus leads to success."

This then is the tension between the flesh and the Spirit. Both the spiritual nature and the sinful nature are pressing for expression. But the outcome of this conflict is peace and joy if we continue to abide in Christ (John 15:1–11). It is by abiding in Christ that we experience a transfomation of moral character that reflects His image; and character is what we take to heaven[7]. Ellen White reminds us, "A character formed according to the divine likeness is the only treasure that we can take from this world to the next."[81] It is not enough to modify our outward behavior.

---

[79] *Steps to Christ*, p. 58.
[80] *Christ's Object Lessons*, pp. 311, 312.
[81] *Christ's Object Lessons*, p. 332.

The very thoughts and intents of the heart are to be transformed through the indwelling of the Holy Spirit. "If the thoughts are wrong, the feelings will be wrong; and the thoughts and feelings combined make up the moral character."[82] To reflect the image of Jesus is to love what He loves and hate what He hates (Heb. 1:9). By the promptings and the enabling power of the indwelling Spirit of God, we are enabled to choose what our thoughts and affections will dwell on—whether on our cherished sins tied to this world or on the love and compassion of God in Christ. So, "let us lay aside every weight, and the sin which so easily ensnares us, and let us run with endurance the race that is set before us" (Heb. 12:1).

Now, while the process of character development is going on in our lives, Christ's perfect character stands before God in the heavenly sanctuary in substitution for our imperfect characters[(1)].[83] As we have noted previously, He is our Substitute and Surety in all things. The truth of these words is then fulfilled in us: "When we are clothed with the righteousness of Christ, we shall have no relish for sin; for Christ will be working with us. We may make mistakes, but we will hate the sin that caused the sufferings of the Son of God."[84]

Through repentance and faith, as we confess our sins, we are accepted in Christ just as if we had never sinned (Eph. 1:6, KJV; Acts 20:20, 21).[85] As we continuously receive Christ and abide in Him, we receive His righteousness, which is imparted to us[(4)].[86] His righteousness permeates our character, and we are infused with His Spirit. All that we need in a righteous character is found in Christ (Col. 2:9, 10; Phil. 4:19; 2 Peter 1:3, 4).[87]

As sanctification by faith progresses, the noble large-hearted graces of the Holy Spirit begin to mature in the character. The inherited and cultivated tendencies to evil are being overcome. Nevertheless, "the closer

---

[82] *In Heavenly Places*, p. 164.

[83] *Steps to Christ*, p. 62; *The Desire of Ages*, p. 762; *Selected Messages*, book 1, p. 367.

[84] *Review and Herald*, March 18, 1890.

[85] *Testimonies for the Church*, vol. 5, p. 472; *Steps to Christ*, p. 62.

[86] *Thoughts from the Mount of Blessing*, p. 18; *Christ's Object Lessons*, p. 327.

[87] *Christ's Object Lessons*, pp. 316, 317, 330.

you come to Jesus, the more faulty you will appear in your own eyes; for your vision will be clearer, and your imperfections will be seen in broad and distinct contrast to His perfect nature. This is evidence that Satan's delusions have lost their power; that the vivifying influence of the Spirit of God is arousing you."[88]

As one moves through life, the punctiliar, one-act sins of 1 John 2:1 will become less and less. The habit of living in the Spirit with Christ will be as though it always has been. Identity with Christ becomes so complete that, when one carries out his or her own impulses, he or she is but carrying out the will of God.[89] The thoughts and feelings that make up moral character (the quality of the soul revealed in conduct) will be in harmony with Christ.[90] We hate what He hates and love what He loves.[91] And so it is established that "faith and love are the essential, powerful, working elements of Christian character."[92]

Character development is the focus of a lifetime, as is sanctification.[93] Sanctification is living in harmony with God's holy law. God is seeking to develop in us a reflection of His character through the indwelling of His word by the Holy Spirit (Ps. 119:11). "None need fail of attaining, *in his sphere*, to perfection of Christian character." There is a reason for this. "In His humanity, perfected by a life of constant resistance of evil, the Savior showed that through co-operation with Divinity, human beings may in this life attain to perfection of character."[94] (See Eph. 5:26, 27; 1 Thess. 5:23.) This means that it is possible to live with our thoughts, feelings, and intentions imbued with the Holy Spirit in harmony with God's holy law

---

[88] *Steps to Christ*, p. 64.

[89] *The Desire of Ages*, p. 668.

[90] *Child Guidance*, p. 161; *Testimonies for the Church*, vol. 5, p. 310; consider Galatians 5:16–25 and Ephesians 2:1–10 in relation to our spiritual and sinful natures. Indeed, in every letter of Paul's he spends much time calling us to live in the attributes of the Spirit. Notice also, that each one deals with thoughts and feelings. And as Ellen White insightfully states, "thoughts and feelings combined make up the moral character." *In Heavenly Places*, p. 164.

[91] *Steps to Christ*, p. 58.

[92] *Our Father Cares*, p. 21.

[93] *Counsels to Parents, Teachers, and Students*, p. 61; *Christ's Object Lessons*, pp. 65, 66.

[94] *Acts of the Apostles*, p. 531, emphasis supplied.

and never fall to the clamors of the lower nature[(6)][95]. The key to victory is humanity imbued with Divinity (2 Peter 1:4).

Imputed and imparted righteousness in balance

When Paul says, "Do not let sin reign in your mortal body, that you should obey it in its lusts" (Rom. 6:12), we must recognize that our sinful natures are ever present to contaminate our good deeds. Ellen White helps us keep everything in perspective. "The Spirit works upon our hearts, drawing out prayers and penitence, praise and thanksgiving.... The religious services, the prayers, the praise, the penitent confession of sin ascend from *true* believers as incense to the heavenly sanctuary, but passing through the corrupt channels of humanity, they are so defiled that unless purified by blood, they can never be of value with God. They ascend not in spotless purity, and unless the Intercessor, who is at God's right hand, presents and purifies all by His righteousness, it is not acceptable to God."[96] It would be well to read this passage in context and meditate on it every day.

As can be seen by the diagram above, the sinful nature remains with us until Jesus returns (1 Cor. 15:53–57)[(7)]. Therefore Ellen White could poignantly say, "We cannot say, 'I am sinless,' till this vile body is changed and fashioned like unto His glorious body. But if we constantly seek to follow Jesus, the blessed hope is ours of standing before the throne of God without spot or wrinkle, or any such thing; complete in Christ, robed in His righteousness and perfection."[97] John Wesley said, "Christ indeed cannot *reign*, where sin *reigns*: neither will he *dwell* where any sin is *allowed*. But he *is* and *dwells* in the heart of every believer, who is fighting against all sin; although it be not yet purified, according to the purification of the

---

[95] *Desire of Ages*, p. 311.
[96] *Selected Messages*, book 1, p. 344, emphasis added; see also *Acts of the Apostles*, p. 561.
[97] *Signs of the Times*, March 23, 1888.

sanctuary."[98] And, as Wesley is often paraphrased as saying, "Sin remains, but it does not reign."[99]

A character "conformed to the image of His Son" (Rom. 8:29) is God's mark of ownership on His people. It is He who gives us repentance and faith for the forgiveness of sin (Acts 5:31). It is He who blots out our sins for His own name's sake (Isa. 43:25). It is He who convicts us of sin in our lives so that we may confess and send all our sins beforehand to judgment (John 16:8; 1 Tim. 5:24, KJV).[100] It is He who gave us the health message so that we may have clear minds to discern spiritual things.[101] Although the Scriptures are replete with injunctions to holy living and character development,[102] our compassionate Savior gave us the Spirit of Prophecy in the writings of Ellen White so that we may know how, in the final phase of the atonement, to deal with sin in our lives.[103]

---

[98] John Wesley, *Sermons on Several Occasions* (London, 1829), vol. 1, p. 121, emphasis in original.

[99] " 'Sin cannot in any kind or degree *exist*, where it does not *reign*.' Absolutely contrary this to all experience, all scripture, all common sense. Resentment of an affront is sin, it is ανομια, disconformity to the law of love. This has existed in me a thousand times. Yet it did not, and does not *reign*" John Wesley, *Sermons on Several Occasions*, I, p. 125).

[100] *Testimonies for the Church*, vol. 5, p. 331. This phrase, "beforehand to judgment," is introduced here as it will be used throughout this volume. Ellen White uses it in multiple places (*The Faith I Live By*, p. 210; *The Great Controversy*, p. 620; *Historical Sketches of the Foreign Missions of the Seventh-day Adventists*, p. 155; etc.), referring to the judgment in the heavenly sanctuary on the antitypical Day of Atonement. It is especially applicable for the final atonement for the living. The sanctuary imagery of the New Testament signifies this phrase is Day of Atonement language. Leviticus chapter four indicates that sin was transferred in figure to the sanctuary, sent on beforehand to the Day of Atonement judgment, the record of sin was forever removed from the sanctuary and the believer on the yearly cycle of the Day of Atonement when sins were blotted out (Lev. 16).

[101] *Counsels on Diet and Foods*, pp. 33, 47–52.

[102] Romans 6; 1 Corinthians 15; 2 Corinthians 5:14–7:1; Galatians 5:16–26. Note that Paul says, "...those who practice such things will not inherit the kingdom of God," v. 21; and exhorts believers to "no longer walk as the rest of the Gentiles walk" (Eph. 4:17–5:16; Phil. 2:1–16; Col. 3; 1 Thess. 5:14–23; and many other similar texts throughout Paul's writings). These texts help us to know what to repent of and claim the victory by faith in Christ's imputed righteousness.

[103] *The Faith I Live By*, p. 210.

Conclusion

The blessing of sanctification by faith is nothing more and nothing less than living in the Spirit with Christ and developing every quality of spiritual life implanted in the soul by His grace. Although a defective character is inherited (Ps. 51:5), there are within us the elements of conscience, the thoughts and the feelings, and the will and the reason, which may be sanctified and enlisted on the side of Christ.[104] With appropriate spiritual nurturing and training under the influence and converting power of the Holy Spirit, a person may grow in character development to the extent that the inherited and cultivated defective character traits will be overcome and the character of Christ will be reflected in the believer.

The lifelong process of sanctification by faith is only completed after probation has closed. Under the sixth of the seven last plagues, the time of trouble is necessary because our "earthliness must be consumed, that the image of Christ may be perfectly reflected," then Jesus returns.[105] Thus does God fulfill what he has assured us—that we are predestined to be "conformed to the image of His Son" (Rom. 8:29). Jesus' promise is: to the one "who overcomes [that is, the one who overcomes the temptation of non-cooperation with Jesus in being transformed into His likeness] I will grant to sit with Me on My throne, as I also overcame and sat down with My Father on His throne" (Rev. 3:21). He is faithful and will bring us through experiences which will lead us to reflect His character if we continue to abide in Him. Then a moral character, which reflects the image of Jesus, is what we take from this world to the next[(7)].[106]

---

[104] *Counsels to Parents, Teachers, and Students*, p. 192.

[105] *The Great Controversy*, p. 621.

[106] *Christ's Object Lessons*, pp. 332, 69.

Chapter 6

Christ—Our Pattern and Example

So, what pattern are we to follow now that we have accepted Jesus as our Savior? I thank God He has not left us in ignorance about how we should respond to His great love for us. He has given us an example in the life of His own Son that we should "walk even as He walked (1 John 2:6) and "follow His steps" (1 Peter 2:21). Paul says that we should love as Christ has loved us in giving Himself for us (Eph. 5:2). Yet, I have learned by experience that, without Christ continually in my life and covering me with His righteousness, I can do nothing that is acceptable to God (John 15:4, 5).

By beholding we become changed

So, the Apostle Paul instructs us to continuously look to Jesus who is both the author (the One who justifies) and the finisher (the One who sancti-fies) of our faith (Heb. 12:2). For it is by "beholding," that is, by study-ing His life as our pattern for Christian living shown to us in both the Bible and the writings of Ellen White, that we are changed into living like Him (2 Cor. 3:18). This is His work of sanctification in us. Sanctification also means being set apart for continuous holy living. Through His grace, Christ sanctifies us by His sacrifice on Calvary, the work of the Holy Spirit, and the Word of God—all working together in harmony for our salvation (Heb. 10:10; 2 Thess. 2:13; John 16:17).

God is not willing that any should perish (2 Peter 3:9). Therefore, God has pulled out all the stops, so to speak, to win our cooperation with Him that He may do for us that which it is impossible for us to do without Him (Jer. 31:3; Ezek. 33:11; John 15:5).

Transformed for sanctified living

God's purpose for us is that we should be changed in nature to the extent that we may live in peace with Him for eternity (Rom. 12:2). Not only that, but it is also that we should rejoice and be glad in His holy presence without fear or shame (Rev. 15:2–4). Through Christ's victory, Adam's failure is to be completely reversed. Yet, God cannot reverse that failure for us without our cooperation.

Let me share with you the high calling of God in Christ Jesus for us to live in harmony with His will. In the writings of Ellen White, I read that Jesus is my pattern and example and that I should follow His example in living the Christian life.[107] I have seen, however, that some turn away from her writings or neglect her counsel because they find her call to follow Christ in holy living hard to take. As I struggled with this myself, I began to realize that Paul's writings also issue strong calls to holy living.[108] Consider this strong call: "Therefore, having these promises, beloved, let us cleanse ourselves from all filthiness of the flesh and spirit, perfecting holiness in the fear of God" (2 Cor. 7:1). Or consider Jesus' strong statement, "Every idle word men may speak, they will give account of it in the day of judgment"

> "*God's purpose for us is that we should be changed in nature to the extent that we may live in peace with Him for eternity.*"

---

[107] Review and Herald, Nov. 20, 1894.

[108] Romans, chapters 3–6; 2 Cor. 5:14 through 7:1; Gal. 5:16–26 (note, in verse 21, that Paul says, "those who practice such things will not inherit the kingdom of God"); Ephesians 4:17–5:16; Philippians 2:1–16; Colossians 3; 1 Thessalonians 5:14–23; and many other like texts as you read through the Scriptures.

(Matt. 12:36). Remember also that Jesus declared we are to be perfect as our Heavenly Father is perfect.[109] Ellen White helped me understand why the conflict sometimes rages between what I want to do and what I know God wants me to do. "The strongest evidence of man's fall from a higher state is the fact that it costs so much to return."[110]

Indeed, there seems to be more written in the New Testament about following in the footsteps of Jesus for sanctified living than there is about His substitutionary work for us. The reason for the overbalance on the former is because of the struggle it takes to "lift" humanity out of the pit of sin into which we have fallen. As Paul wrote, "We do not wrestle against flesh and blood, but against principalities, against powers, against the rulers of the darkness of this age" (Eph. 6:12).

For those who view the writings of Ellen White as irrelevant or who avoid the biblical injunctions to sanctified living, let me remind you of the balance found in both the Bible and Ellen White's writings.[111] The following statement brings everything into perspective. Jesus "is our pattern.... He is a perfect and holy example, given for us to imitate. We cannot equal the pattern; but we shall not be approved of God if we do not copy it and, *according to the ability which God has given*, resemble it."[112]

As we seek to follow our blessed Savior in all that He would have us do, we need to always embrace the encouragement that "man's obedience can be made perfect only by the incense of Christ's righteousness" in the heavenly sanctuary.[113] This means that, because He is the representative man, His righteousness stands in place of our fallen human nature. As Ellen White wrote, "His life stands for the life of men."[114] What a blessing!

May God help us not to follow the example of Ahab. Because Ahab wanted to go to war against Syria over Ramoth, a piece of land in Gilead,

---

[109] Matthew 5:48; see our Savior's entire discourse in Matthew, chapters 5 through 7.

[110] E. G. White, *Revival and Beyond* (1972), p. 60.

[111] Romans 8 and 12; 2 Corinthians 6:15–7:1; Galatians 5:16–26; Ephesians 3:14–19; 4:17–5:33; Philippians 4:8; Colossians 3:1–4:6; 1 Thessalonians 5:14–23; etc.

[112] *Testimonies for the Church*, vol. 2, p. 549, emphasis added.

[113] *Acts of the Apostles*, p. 532.

[114] *The Desire of Ages*, p. 762.

he asked Jehoshaphat king of Judah to join him in the battle. Jehoshaphat asked Ahab to inquire what the word of the Lord might say concerning their battle plans. Ahab brought in his prophets, and with one voice they all said good things about the outcome of the war. Jehoshaphat was a bit suspicious and asked Ahab if there were any other prophets. Ahab responded, "There is still one man ... but I hate him, because he never prophesies good concerning me, but always evil" (2 Chron. 18:7). When we are living outside of God's will as was Ahab, it will be natural for us to hate either the message or the messenger.

God has not called us to a standard that is impossible for humans to reach. If it seems that way, maybe we are focused on the wrong goal. We need to know whether we are looking to self or to Jesus. Let me explain. Jesus told us that, without Him, we can do nothing (John 15:5). And Ellen White said, "He who is trying to become holy by his own works in keeping the law, is attempting an impossibility."[115] Yes, we can continue to go to church and all the while be in despair and without hope in our struggle to be a Christian. Or, we can put the struggle out of our minds to have some semblance of peace in our hearts. That is the saddest situation, for our wonderful Savior says, "Peace I leave with you, My peace I give to you; ... Let not your heart be troubled, neither let it be afraid" (John 14:27). Nonetheless, if we continue to look to ourselves and hold to "the principle that man can save himself by his own works," we "have no barrier against sin."[116]

There are other verses which help us understand the Christian walk of life in following Jesus as our Pattern and Example. When we were baptized, we rose from that watery grave to walk in newness of life (Rom. 6:3–6). Peter tells us, "Christ also suffered for us, leaving us an example, that you should follow His steps" (1 Peter 2:21). When we received Christ as Savior, we were totally dependent upon Him for the forgiveness of sin and for the power of His indwelling Spirit to live for Him. Now Paul says

---

[115] *Steps to Christ*, p. 59.
[116] *The Desire of Ages*, p. 35.

that, *in the same way* we received Christ as our Savior, we are also to live in Him (Col. 2:6, 7).

Conclusion

Through Jesus we are adopted into the family of God to live like a child of the King, to follow His example and live as He lived (Rom. 8:14–16; Gal. 4:4–7). It is said that "like begets like" and that "deep calls unto deep" (Ps. 42:7). It is evident that only those of like character can live in harmony. "Can two walk together, unless they are agreed?" (Amos 3:3). God has promised not only justification but also sanctification to bring us into harmony with Heaven so that we will not be ashamed when Jesus returns. How great is our merciful Judge in compassion, wisdom, and power, that we, all undeserving, may be fitted through His grace to live with Him for eternity. The following admonition from Ellen White is encouraging as we live for and with Christ.

"We are sons and daughters of God. In order to know how to behave ourselves circumspectly, we must follow where Christ leads the way.... Our only safety is to follow where the steps of the Master lead the way, to trust for protection implicitly to Him who says, 'Follow me.' Our constant prayer should be, 'Hold up my goings in thy path, O Lord, that my footsteps slip not' (Ps. 17:5)."[117]

Jesus, our Wonderful Judge, wants us to be free from guilt, and He wants us to experience the joy and blessing of right doing (John 15:11).[118] Let us not chafe at the word "obedience," for to do so reveals the natural heart. Our natural inclinations are always ready to rebel against God. But, having accepted Christ as our Savior, He has become our pattern and example in living the Christian life. When Mephibosheth came to dine at

---

[117] *Sons and Daughters of God*, p. 154.

[118] "Christ is ready to pardon all who come to Him confessing their sins. To the tried, struggling soul is spoken the word, 'Let him take hold of My strength, that he may make peace with Me, and he shall make peace with Me.'" (Ms. 113, 1902); see also *Thoughts from the Mount of Blessing*, p. 146.

David's table, he had to learn how to act in the presence of the king. So it is in living the Christian life. We "grow in grace" (2 Peter 3:18, KJV) that, when He returns, we will be prepared to meet Him in peace. John wrote: "Everyone who has this hope in Him purifies himself, just as He is pure" (1 John 3:3). Therefore, Christ has shown us how to practice living for heaven. He has given us a perfect example of how to live in love to God and our fellow human beings.[119] It is He who "leads me in the paths of righteousness for His name's sake" (Ps. 23:3).

---

[119] *The Seventh-day Adventist Bible Commentary*, vol. 7, p. 925; see also *The Seventh-day Adventist Bible Commentary*, vol. 7, p. 930; and *Testimonies for the Church*, vol. 5, p. 422.

Chapter 7

The Holy Spirit—Our Helper and Our Guide

After Christ's resurrection and ascension, He was inaugurated as our High Priest in the heavenly sanctuary. When Jesus was thus glorified, the Holy Spirit was poured out on the believers on the Day of Pentecost (John 7:39). Peter said, "Therefore being exalted to the right hand of God, and having received from the Father the promise of the Holy Spirit, He poured out this which you now see and hear" (Acts 2:33). It was from that day on that the believers were imbued with the Holy Spirit. The fulfillment of that promise of the Holy Spirit to be our Comforter, Helper, and Guide is the same for us today. "For the promise is to you and to your children, and to all who are afar off, as many as the Lord our God will call" (Acts 2:39).

"Now we have received, not the spirit of the world, but the Spirit who is from God, that we might know the things that have been freely given to us by God" (1 Cor. 2:12). Without the Holy Spirit we would be ignorant of God's plan of salvation through Christ our righteousness (John 15:26). It is the Holy Spirit, whom God has given to us to be with us and in us that guides us to a saving knowledge of Jesus (John 14:17). The essence of living the Christian life is being born of the Holy Spirit and having the Spirit abiding in us daily. The indwelling Spirit testifies to us that we are the children of God, and, if we do "not have the Spirit of Christ," we are not His (Rom. 8:9, 16).

In both *Selected Messages*, book 1, page 367, and *Steps to Christ*, page 62, after clearly explaining how Christ's life stands in the place of our life before God, Ellen White passes along two promises. The first is: "Our only ground of hope is in the righteousness of Christ imputed to us, and in that wrought by His Spirit working in and through us."[120] The second is: "In the great and measureless gift of the Holy Spirit are contained all of heaven's resources."[121] The Trinity or —God the Father, Son, and Holy Spirit—is involved in our salvation and in our inheritance of the kingdom that Adam lost.[122] Jesus said, "I will pray the Father, and He will give you another Helper," or "Comforter" (John 14:16). The word "another" means another of the same kind—the same essence—to be to each of us as Jesus was to His disciples. The Holy Spirit is Christ's representative on earth and our Divine Helper and Guide. A beautiful hymn says, "Spirit of God, my Teacher be, showing the things of Christ to me."[123]

The work of the Holy Spirit for us

The human condition apart from Christ is degenerate and ruined. Paul says, "For we know that the law is spiritual, but I am carnal, sold under sin." And again, "For I know that in me (that is, in my flesh) nothing good dwells" (Rom. 7:14, 18). Restoration from our degenerate condition starts solely from God's great love and mercy for us in allowing Jesus to be clothed with human form and nature. His holy living and dying in our place has reconciled us to God (2 Cor. 5:19). Since the time of Adam's fall

---

[120] *Steps to Christ*, p. 63.

[121] *Christ's Object Lessons*, p. 419.

[122] Though Ellen White may never have used the term "Trinity" because of certain false assumptions attached to the term in other churches, she did refer to "the Father, the Son, and the Holy Ghost" as "the eternal Godhead" (Ms. 45, 1904), and she did repeatedly refer to the *three-ness* of God in such terms as the "three living persons of the Heavenly Trio" (Ms. 21, 1906), "the three great powers" (Ms. 57, 1900; Ms. 11, 1901; Ms. 30, 1902; Ms. 118, 1902; Lt. 102, 1903; Lt. 129, 1903; Ms. 190, 1903; Lt. 1, 1904; Lt. 53, 1904; Ms. 159, 1904; Ms. 54, 1905; Ms. 66, 1905; Ms. 181, 1905; Ms. 187, 1905; Ms. 191, 1905; Ms. 182, 1907; Ms. 183, 1907; Ms. 37, 1908), and the "three great Worthies in/ of heaven" (Ms. 95, 1906; Ms. 145, 1906). She also wrote: "Three distinct agencies, the Father, the Son, and the Holy Ghost, work together for human beings. They are united in the work of making the church on earth like the church in heaven" (Ms. 27a, 1900).

[123] Eliza E. Hewitt, "More About Jesus," *Seventh-day Adventist Hymnal* (1985), hymn no. 245.

until the restoration of all things, the plan of redemption has been committed to the Son, our Lord and Savior Jesus Christ (1 Cor. 15:24, 25). Ellen White wrote, "The world has been committed to Christ, and through Him has come every blessing from God to the fallen race."[124] But the work of Christ for us would not be complete without the Holy Spirit's work for us and in us. Indeed, it is faith in Christ's work for us that brings the Holy Spirit to us (Gal. 3:1, 2, 14), and the Holy Spirit, our Helper, guides us to Christ (John 16:13–15). The ravages of sin have well nigh obliterated the image of God in us. But God has promised that, through His Holy Spirit, He "will restore to you the years that the locust hath eaten" (Joel 2:25, KJV).

It is the Holy Spirit who guides us into all truth. Jesus said, "When He, the Spirit of truth, has come, He will guide you into all truth" (John 16:13). He was not sent to testify of Himself but to make known to us what the Father and the Son have done for our salvation. It is astounding and worthy of our greatest praise and gratitude that the work of redemption for rebellious humanity is accomplished by the harmonious activity of the Trinity in the recovery of what was lost in Adam. "When we were baptized 'in the name of the Father, and of the Son, and of the Holy Ghost,' these three great powers pledged themselves to work in our behalf as we strove to live the new life in Christ" (Lt. 200, 1902).

In order to participate in the recovery of what was lost through Adam, we must experience the new birth. In other words, we must be born into the family of God. This is accomplished by the Holy Spirit's work for us and in us. It is the will of God that we should be born into His family (John 1:12, 13). Once we are spiritually reborn, we are filled with the Holy Spirit and "grow in the grace and knowledge of our Lord and Savior Jesus Christ" (2 Peter 3:18).

It is the Spirit that reveals the way of salvation to us. He is constantly wooing us with His everlasting love (Jer. 31:3) so we will look to Jesus as the author and finisher of our faith (Heb. 12:2). Indeed, without the

---

[124] *The Desire of Ages*, p. 210.

Spirit, we would not have faith to look to Jesus for salvation. Jesus said that the Holy Spirit would guide us into all truth, for Jesus is the way, the truth, and the life (John 14:6). The only truth of Scripture is the truth as it is in Jesus, and the Holy Spirit creates a love of God's truth in our hearts. To "not receive the love of the truth" (2 Thess. 2:10) is to reject the Holy Spirit, which then leads to the unpardonable sin—a very serious condition indeed. However, if we do not resist the Holy Spirit, He will not only be our Helper to help us have faith in Jesus, but He will also serve as our Guide to lead us to Jesus.

The work of the Holy Spirit in us

The health message, which God has given to the Seventh-day Adventist Church through the writings of Ellen White, in conjunction with the sciences of modern medicine, helps us to understand how the Holy Spirit works in and through us. When I was preparing for my Master of Public Health (MPH) degree, I came across a statement in my textbook on anatomy and physiology that really astounded me. It reads in part, "The cerebral cortex—and therefore our thoughts and emotions—can, by way of the hypothalamus, influence the functioning of all our billions of cells. In short, the brain has two-way contact with every tissue of the body.... The state of the body influences mental processes, which in turn, influence the state of the body."[125] Then I read the following from Ellen White, "The brain nerves which *communicate with the entire system* are the only medium through which Heaven can communicate to man and affect his inmost life."[126] It is obvious then that, *through our thoughts and feelings,* which make up our moral character,[127] God not only communicates to us His plan of salvation but also, through the Holy Spirit, He imprints in us His holy law (2 Cor. 3:3, 18; Heb. 8:10).

---

[125] Catherine Parker Anthony, *Textbook of Anatomy and Physiology* (1967), p. 500.

[126] *Testimonies for the Church*, vol. 2, p. 347, emphasis added.

[127] *Testimonies for the Church*, vol. 5, p. 310.

I took my MPH because of my interest in the Seventh-day Adventist health message and how it influences our relationship with Christ. The Apostle John connected the health of body and soul when he wrote, "Beloved, I pray that you may prosper in all things and be in health, just as your soul prospers" (3 John 2). And Paul says, "Do you not know that your body is the temple of the Holy Spirit who is in you, whom you have from God, and you are not your own? For you were bought at a price; therefore glorify God in your body and in your spirit, which are God's" (1 Cor. 6:19, 20). The chapter on diet and spirituality in *Counsels on Diet and Foods* explains this topic very nicely. It says, "A close sympathy exists between the physical and the moral nature."[128] Artificial stimulants and intemperance in all aspects of life have "a benumbing influence upon the brain, making it impossible to appreciate eternal things."[129] It is my belief that God gave us the health message so that we might be advantaged in our relationship with Him.

The Spirit sanctifies the Word in us

It is the Holy Spirit that sanctifies us through faith in Jesus (1 Peter 1:2). Just as Jesus could say, "The words that I speak to you are spirit, and they are life" (John 6:63), so also could He say, "Sanctify them by Your truth. Your word is truth" (John 17:17). The close relation between the words of Christ and the Holy Spirit is illustrated by the parallelism of Proverbs 1:23, "Surely I will pour out my spirit on you; I will make my words known to you."

The seed that causes spiritual growth in our lives is the word of God (1 Peter 1:23). Jesus used agricultural metaphors to teach us about the process of the Christian life. The early rain on the fields gives life to the grain. The latter rain brings it to maturity. In the same way, the Holy Spirit

---

[128] *Counsels on Diet and Foods*, p. 43.
[129] *Counsels on Diet and Foods*, p. 48.

working in our hearts leads us to behold the righteousness and mercy of our Lord Jesus Christ and transforms our character. It is through the Spirit that the "righteous requirement of the law" is "fulfilled in us" (Rom. 8:4). "As we seek God for the Holy Spirit, it will work in us meekness, humbleness of mind, a conscious dependence upon God for the perfecting latter rain. If we pray for the blessing in faith, we shall receive it as God has promised."[130]

The Holy Spirit, as the representative of Christ on earth, is everything to us. Paul says, "If anyone does not have the Spirit of Christ, he is not His" (Rom. 8:9). It is the Holy Spirit in us that draws from our hearts praise, adoration, and worship to God. Thus, by the Spirit, we worship God in "spirit and in truth" (John 4:23, 24). It is by the Spirit that we overcome sin in our lives and that our names are retained in the book of life (Rev. 3:5). Paul says, "If by the Spirit you put to death the deeds of the body, you will live. For as many as are led by the Spirit of God, these are sons of God" (Rom. 8:13, 14). Without the Holy Spirit in us, we are still in spiritual darkness and cannot discern the things of God's great salvation for us (1 Cor. 2:14–16).

The Spirit and unity

Not only does the Holy Spirit work in and through us individually, but the Holy Spirit, as Christ's representative on earth, directs the affairs of the church. Indeed, the church is also the temple of the Holy Spirit. We often use 1 Corinthians 3:16 to refer to our individual bodies as temples of the Holy Spirit, but it may also mean the community of believers, for the "you" in the verse is plural. Jesus said the Holy Spirit dwells with *you* (plural) and will be in *you* (singular) (John 14:17). Paul then gives the warning, "If anyone defiles the temple of God, God will destroy him. For the temple of God is holy, which *temple* you [plural] are" (2 Cor. 3:17, emphasis

---

[130] *Testimonies for Ministers*, p. 508.

added; see also Eph. 2:19–22). We need to be sensitive to the working of the Holy Spirit in and through the church of Christ. Ellen White cautions,

> "*The Holy Spirit brings us into harmony with God's character as revealed in His holy law. It is this harmony with God that leads us into sanctification by faith and unity within the church.*"

"The Lord lays upon no man a message that will discourage and dishearten the church."[131]

How grateful we can be for the health counsel from Ellen White that helps us appreciate and accept the work of the Holy Spirit for our salvation individually and for God's church. The Holy Spirit brings us into harmony with God's character as revealed in His holy law. It is this harmony with God that leads us into sanctification by faith and unity within the church.

---

[131] *Testimonies for Ministers*, p. 22.

CHRIST OUR RIGHTEOUSNESS AND THE SANCTUARY

Chapter 8

The Earthly Sanctuary—
Made After the Pattern

To understand Christ our righteousness and the sanctuary, it is necessary to understand something about the earthly sanctuary that was made according to the pattern that God showed Moses on Mount Sinai (Heb. 8:5). Jesus is "the Lamb of God who takes away the sin of the world" (John 1:29). He is also "the Lamb slain from the foundation of the world" (Rev. 13:8). The central focus of the earthly sanctuary service was the lamb, which was offered "day by day continually" upon the altar of burnt offering (Exod. 29:38, 39). The material covered in this section will provide rudimentary knowledge for some, and it will be a review for others.

The structure

First, we will look at the structure of the sanctuary and its services.[132] Psalm 77:13 says, "Thy way, O God, is in the sanctuary" (KJV).[133] The Septuagint, the Greek translation of the Old Testament used when Jesus walked the earth, agrees with this rendering of the text. Additionally, the Hebrew word *qôdesh*, which means "holy," can also be rendered "sanctuary" (see Exod. 28:43; 29:30). Certainly God's way of revealing Himself to us in regard to

---

[132] See Exodus 25:1–31:17 for the details of the earthly sanctuary.

[133] Several translations, including the KJV as well as the Septuagint render this text "in the sanctuary." See also Psalm 63:2; 134:2.

our salvation is in the sanctuary, for He told Moses to make a sanctuary that He may dwell among His people (Exod. 25:8). Not only would God dwell among His people, but He would show them His intentions for the salvation of humanity through the sanctuary rituals. All was to be done according to the pattern that God showed Moses when he met with Him in the mount. As other nations would see the blessings of God on His people, they would be led to acknowledge the true God (Deut. 4:5, 6). Through the sacrificial offerings, Christ would be exalted as the coming Savior of the world.[134]

An understanding of the sanctuary and its rituals will greatly enhance our understanding of the marvelous salvation we have in Christ our Lord. The sanctuary was of unique measurements. It consisted of two apartments, or rooms. The first of these was twice as long as it was wide and its height was the same as its width. This first apartment had various names, including the tabernacle, the tent of meeting (or "the tent of the congregation," KJV), and the holy place (Exod. 25:9; 39:32; 26:33). The second apartment was of the same width and height as the first apartment, but it was half its length. Thus, it formed a cube. What separated the first apartment from the second was not a wall but a curtain. The curtain was also called a veil, or a hanging. This second, inner apartment was called the most holy place (Exod. 26:34), the holy of holies, the holiest of all, or, on the Day of Atonement, simply "the holy place" (Lev. 16). The whole edifice was called the sanctuary, and it faced east. The entrance was through a veil, which was also called a curtain or a hanging. Thus, the hanging between the holy and the most holy place was called the "second veil" (Heb. 9:3).

In front of the sanctuary was the laver of washing, and in front of the laver was the altar of burnt offerings. The whole area was enclosed by an outer court of white linen.

On the inside of the first apartment were three articles of furniture. To the left was the seven-branched golden lampstand called the menorah. To the right was the table of showbread with twelve flat loaves of unleavened

---

[134] *Christ's Object Lessons*, pp. 289, 290.

bread on it. Directly ahead and just in front of the second veil separating the two apartments was the altar of incense.

Inside the separation veil was the most holy place. It had only one article of furniture—the ark of the covenant (Exod. 26:33).[135] The ark of the covenant was 52 inches long, 31 inches wide, and 31 inches high. It was overlaid with pure gold both inside and out.[136] A lid of pure gold covered the ark, and attached to the lid were two cherubim of pure gold facing each other. One wing of each angel touched above and the other wing extended over the lid of the ark (Exod. 25:20). The faces of the cherubim were looking downward toward the cover, or mercy seat, of the ark.

There were other items within the sanctuary that assisted in the priestly ministry. However, for the purposes of this book, these are the only ones that we will consider.

The services

The central service throughout the year was twofold. Every day the morning and evening sacrifice was offered on the altar of burnt offerings in the courtyard before the entrance veil of the tabernacle. The only thing between the entrance veil and the altar was the laver of washing where the priests performed their cleansing and purification rituals before entering the sanctuary.[137]

Simultaneously with the offering of the morning and evening sacrifice was the offering of incense on the altar of incense in front of the second veil between the holy and most holy place. Both of these offerings were morning and evening daily offerings (2 Chron. 13:11), also referred to as

---

[135] Also called the "ark of the testimony" (Exod. 25:10; 25:16; 26:33; Rev. 11:19, KJV).

[136] This measurement is according to the royal cubit of Egypt since Moses was trained in the court of Egypt and the Israelite slaves built much of the royal structures (see *The Seventh-day Adventist Bible Commentary*, vol. 1, pp. 636, 637).

[137] See *The Seventh-day Adventist Bible Commentary*, vol. 1, pp. 693–710, for an understanding of the services of the earthly sanctuary.

"continual offerings." The fire on these altars was to never go out. By sacrifice and incense the Israelites approached God and were made acceptable to Him.[138]

Although there were individual burnt offerings and sin offerings, as well as other purification offerings, these twofold offerings were central to the worship services of the ancient Israelites. Indeed, the morning and evening offerings became the time of morning and evening worship and prayer for the Israelites. One example of this is the prophet Daniel. As his habit was, he prayed toward the temple in Jerusalem at the time when the offerings would have taken place—even though the temple had been destroyed (Dan. 6:10; 9:21). Another example comes from the temple services in Jerusalem at the time of Christ. Luke records that Zacharias' "lot fell to burn incense when he went into the temple of the Lord. And the whole multitude of the people was praying outside at the hour of incense" (Luke 1:9, 10).

Other services of significance for our purposes here were the yearly sabbaths, the Passover, the wave sheaf, Pentecost, the blowing of trumpets, the Day of Atonement, and the Feast of Tabernacles. Although there were six yearly sabbaths in the law of Moses (see Lev. 23, for days of "no customary work"), a seventh was added at the time of the Maccabees when the temple was rededicated after its restoration from desecration by Antiochus Epiphanes. Jesus went up to Jerusalem at the Feast of Dedication (John 10:22, 23).

The Israelites were required, however, to attend only three of these yearly feasts at the temple in Jerusalem—the Feast of Unleavened Bread (which included Passover), Pentecost, and the Feast of Tabernacles (Deut. 16:16).

---

[138] *The Faith I Live By*, p. 197.

The sacrifice, the law, and the priest

It is difficult to identify which is the most important aspect of the earthly sanctuary services—the law or the lamb. Without the law of Ten Commandments placed within the sacred ark of the covenant, there would be no formalized knowledge of sin. Without the Lamb, there would be no remedy for sin. Thus, the sanctuary shows that law and grace are two inseparable aspects of redemption.[139] The way of salvation is not law *or* grace but law *and* grace, working in harmony for the restoration of the human race.

However important as are the law and the lamb, there would be no application of the atonement without the priest. Thus, we see that the sanctuary service is a perfect unit, or system of truth. It illustrates how an infinite, pure, and holy God can redeem His people to Himself. By it, He can retain the holiness of His character in justice and mercy while still dwelling with His people who are marred by sin. In Romans 3:19–31, Paul explains the fulfillment of this plan for our salvation: that God "might be just and the justifier of the one who has faith in Jesus" (Rom. 3:26).

The burnt offering and the sin—or purification—offering were the most frequently mentioned offerings.[140] The continuous burnt offering was to be present on the altar every day of the week, all day and all year long. It was never to go out. At the times when this offering was renewed morning and evening, the priests offered incense on the altar of incense before the second veil. Behind this veil was the "ark of the testimony" containing the Ten Commandments (Exod. 26:33; 30:7, 8; Lev. 6:12, 13). The blood of all burnt offerings was first sprinkled against the northern side of the altar of burnt offerings, and the remainder was poured out at the base of the altar (Lev. 1:5, 11, 15). Through the purification offering (also called the sin offering), sin was transferred in figure to the sanctuary.[141]

---

[139] See *The Seventh-day Adventist Bible Commentary*, vol. 1, pp. 694, 695.

[140] Martin T. Pröbstle, *Where God and I Meet: The Sanctuary* (2013), chapter 5.

[141] *The Great Controversy*, p. 418.

The blood was sprinkled before the veil that separated the holy place from the most holy place. This record of forgiven sin was symbolically removed from the sanctuary on the Day of Atonement (Lev. 16:33).

Other sacrifices, which related to the entire life cycle and existence of the Israelite, were offered throughout the year. Nonetheless, the Day of Atonement sacrificial service was the most solemn service of all. The continuous burnt offerings did not cease on the Day of Atonement. However, other special sacrifices were also offered. Of particular interest to the Israelites was the Lord's goat, which was used to make final atonement for Israel through the removal of sin from sinners. The other goat, Azazel (Lev. 16:8, NET), symbolically carried the record of the sins of Israel away from the Israelites into the "wilderness."

This removal, or blotting out, of sin, removed the sins of Israel as far from the people as the "east is from the west" (Ps. 103:12). In another figure of speech, these sins were cast "into the depths of the sea" (Micah 7:19) on the Day of Atonement. Scripture knows of no other way that God removed Israel's sins. It behooves us to remember the sanctuary imagery when we talk about our sins being cast "into the depths of the sea."

The believing Israelite

The believing Israelite had a knowledge of sin because of the Ten Commandments, which were housed in the ark of the testimony and placed in the center of the Most Holy Place of the sanctuary. Through the statutes and judgments written by Moses the Israelite could understand the far-reaching application of this law (Lev. 26:46; Mal. 4:4).[142]

Besides the Ten Commandment rules of life, Moses wrote instructions to help the believing Israelite know how to be restored to God's favor

---

[142] "The statutes and judgments specifying the duty of man to his fellow-men, were full of important instruction, defining and simplifying the principles of the moral law, for the purpose of increasing religious knowledge, and of preserving God's chosen people distinct and separate from idolatrous nations" (*Review and Herald*, May 6, 1875).

should he sin. The first provision was the morning and evening sacrifice. At these times, the Israelite would pray towards the sanctuary in worship and confession of sin. He placed his faith in the blood of the offering, the ministration of the priest, and the incense ascending from the altar of incense before the second veil. Daniel's prayer is an illustration of the faith of an Israelite in the daily sanctuary services.

The second provision was the sin offering which the believer himself brought to the sanctuary. Various other offerings were made. But, the key point is that day by day the believer's faith was in (1) the condition of the animal to be sacrificed without spot or blemish (Lev. 1:10, etc.), (2) the blood of the sacrifice, which was poured out at the base of the altar and ministered in the holy place before the veil and on the horns of the altar of incense (Lev. 4), and (3) the ministration of the priest who was sanctified and holy. Indeed, the sacrifices, the priesthood, and everything connected with the sanctuary were considered holy (see, for example, Exod. 39:41; Lev. 21:7).

On the yearly cycle of the Day of Atonement, the believer spent the day in deep heart-searching, knowing that all his sins had gone beforehand to the sanctuary through the daily services. And now, on this day, the sanctuary was ready to be cleansed, and sin, to be blotted out. His faith was in the sacrifice and the ministration of the High Priest. If he had done his part and the High Priest was doing his part, he knew that his sins would be removed as far as the east is from the west and that he would be sealed.[143] What a blessedness for the repenting believing Israelite on the Day of Atonement!

---

[143] Pröbstle, p. 67.

Chapter 9

The Heavenly Sanctuary— the One the Lord Made

In trying to understand the heavenly sanctuary, it is essential to explore what God has revealed to us in Scripture and the Spirit of Prophecy. As it is written, "We must know Him as He reveals Himself."[144] We cannot add to or subtract from what is written (Rev. 22:18). There are many things that God has not revealed to us, but what He has revealed is for all of us and for every generation (Deut. 29:29).

The Scriptures reveal that there is a temple in heaven, which is referred to as the throne room of God (Rev. 4; 11:19). Yet, a temple in heaven cannot contain the glory and majesty of God (2 Chron. 2:6), and the earthly sanctuary was but a faint shadow and a replication of the majesty of the heavenly sanctuary. Nevertheless, God would have us understand the heavenly by the pattern that He showed Moses in the mount from which the earthly was built (Heb. 8:1–6).

The New Testament writers had the temple structure in their midst until it was destroyed in A.D. 70 by the Roman General Titus. As Jews, they would understand the way of salvation as it relates to the sanctuary. John says, "The law was given through Moses, but grace and truth came through Jesus Christ" (John 1:17). Since the laws that governed the services of the sanctuary (which pointed the way to salvation) found their fulfillment in the grace and truth of Christ, the New Testament writers— especially Paul—were constantly showing how the order of things had

---

[144] *The Ministry of Healing*, p. 409.

changed from the earthly sanctuary to the heavenly (e.g., Heb. 7:12). Thus, the Jews continually accused Paul of destroying their traditions (Acts 21:28).

The structure

The most explicit description of the heavenly sanctuary is the pattern that was given to Moses at Mount Sinai (Exod. 25:9; Heb. 8:5). Although the pattern was a tent, it was also called the temple of God (Ps. 27). Micah referred to the heavenly dwelling of God as His holy temple (Micah 1:2, 3). Isaiah saw the Most Holy Place, the throne room of God, in heaven (Isa. 6). And, Habakkuk called for reverence because of the majesty of God's presence in His holy heavenly temple (Hab. 2:20). In the Most Holy Place is the ark of the testimony (Rev. 11:19). Over the ark are covering, or guardian, cherubim. Before his fall, Lucifer was one of the cherubim (Ezek. 28:16). God's presence is manifest between and above the cherubim (Exod. 25:18, 22; Ps. 99:1; Heb. 9:5). In the heavenly sanctuary, God sits enthroned, encircled by angels and heavenly beings (Dan. 7:9, 10; Rev. 4 and 5).

The tabernacle that God revealed to Moses is also called the "temple" and the "sanctuary." Because the Israelites had this physical structure in their midst, they had an opportunity to understand the heavenly in relation to it. Thus, we see—especially in the book of Revelation—items in the heavenly sanctuary: the ark of the Ten Commandments in the temple of God in heaven (Rev. 11:19; cf. Exod. 26:33, 34; 34:28, 29), the seven candlesticks (Rev. 1:20; 4:5), and the altar of incense (Rev. 4:5; 8:3). The outer court is left out, for this is the place of the sacrifice of the Lamb, which was fulfilled in Jesus (Rev. 11:2) on earth.[145] Then we see the Lamb, as it had been slain, in the throne room of God that is in the heavenly sanctuary (Rev. 5:6). Indeed, it is well to understand the sanctuary as a principle of interpretation when studying the whole of the

---

[145] Jesus, as the "Lamb of God" died for our sins on this earth.

New Testament. It is the subject of the sanctuary that reveals a "complete system of truth, connected and harmonious."[146] As Dr. Fernando Canali stated in his class, "The heavenly sanctuary is the organizing principle of Seventh-day Adventist theology."[147]

The services

The services of the earthly sanctuary lead us to focus on the work of Christ our High Priest and Savior in the heavenly sanctuary. From the Gospels to Revelation, Christ is referred to as the "Lamb of God" (John 1:29; cf. Rev. 5:6; 7:17; 22:3). In the earthly service, a lamb was offered on the altar of burnt offering both evening and morning (Exod. 29:38, 39). It was a continual intercession of blood that provided atonement for the sins of Israel. The blood of the sacrifice was poured out at the base of the altar, signifying Christ's sacrifice for us in this world. Blood from the sin offering was taken into the Holy Place of the sanctuary and put on the horns of the altar of incense, while some of that blood was sprinkled before the veil where the Ten Commandments in the Most Holy Place pointed out sin. So Christ has entered the heavenly sanctuary presenting His blood in behalf of New Testament believers (Heb. 9:11, 12). Christ has fulfilled the earthly sanctuary rituals that pointed toward His saving grace under the New Covenant.[148]

The sacrifice, the law, and the priest

The Apostle Peter refers to Christ as the Lamb without spot or blemish that died as the sinner's Substitute (1 Peter 1:19). Christ, in his humanity

---

[146] *The Great Controversy*, p. 423.

[147] Class notes from *Principles and Methods of Theology*, Andrews University presented by Fernando Canali, PhD, Winter Quarter, 1991, Feb. 21 and March 12.

[148] *Patriarchs and Prophets*, p. 330.

was pure, undefiled, and sinless—a perfect sacrifice and a perfectly sinless human being (Heb. 7:26). If He were not, He Himself would have needed a savior. This could never be if He were to be our Savior. Jesus' life was totally in harmony with the perfect law of God. His state of being, His inner thoughts and feelings were as pure as the spiritual intent of the Ten Commandments (John 14:30; 2 Cor. 5:21).

> In taking upon Himself man's nature in its fallen condition, Christ did not in the least participate in its sin.... He was touched with the feeling of our infirmities, and was in all points tempted like as we are. And yet He knew no sin.... Could Satan in the least particular have tempted Christ to sin, ... divine wrath would have come upon Christ as it came upon Adam. Christ and the church would have been without hope. We should have no misgivings in regard to the perfect sinlessness of the human nature of Christ.[149]

The priest of old had to be holy and perfectly forgiven if he were to minister in behalf of the Israelites. In like manner, Jesus is a perfect High Priest, not only according to the high priest of the earthly sanctuary but also according to the order of Melchizedek (Heb. 7). It is important to remember this lest we become confused as to the fulfillment He achieved. He is the Priest of all priests. Every sacrifice and every priestly function is fulfilled in Him.[150] "For Christ has not entered the holy places made with hands, which are copies of the true, but into heaven itself, now to appear in the presence of God for us" (Heb. 9:24).

Ellen White admonishes us to look up. "Lift up your eyes toward the heavenly sanctuary, where Christ your Mediator stands before the Father to present your prayers as fragrant incense, mingled with his own merit and spotless righteousness. You are invited to come, to ask, to seek, to

---

[149] *Selected Messages*, book 1, p. 256.
[150] *The Seventh-day Adventist Bible Commentary*, vol. 1, p. 694.

knock, and you are assured that you will not come in vain."[151] In the sanctuary above, the one that the Lord "pitched, and not man" (Heb. 8:2, KJV), we have a High Priest whose name is "the LORD OUR RIGHTEOUSNESS" (Jer. 33:16). He is Himself the lamb, Himself the priest.[152]

The believer

The New Testament believer, through faith in Christ, experiences the new birth. "And as Moses lifted up the serpent in the wilderness, even so must the Son on Man be lifted up, that whoever believes in Him should not perish but have eternal life" (John 3:14, 15). The first step in the new birth comes through looking to Christ crucified (Gal. 3:1, 2). Without the new birth, that is, being born of the Spirit and of water, we cannot comprehend the things of God (John 3:3–6; 1 Cor. 2:12, 13). Through the new birth we participate in the New Covenant that Christ has secured for us. Of Jesus it is written:

> "Lo, I have arrived to do your Sovereign will, O God." He takes away the first [the Old Covenant] in order that He may establish the second [the New Covenant].… Now the Holy Spirit also testifies to us in that He said beforehand, "This [is] the covenant that I Myself will covenant to them after those days," says the Lord, "Inscribing My laws upon their hearts, I will imprint them upon their intentions. And their sins and lawless deeds I will by no means remember any more." … Having therefore, brothers, freedom in speaking into the entrance way of the Sanctuary (by means of the blood of Jesus), which He instituted for us—a new and living way—through the veil (this veil is His flesh);

---

[151] *Christian Education*, pp. 127, 128.
[152] *The Desire of Ages*, p. 25.

and [having] a great priest over the house of God; let us draw near with a true heart in full confidence of faith (having our hearts sprinkled from an evil conscience, and our bodies washed with pure water). (Heb. 10:9, 15–17, 19–22, author's translation).

By faith in Christ, we are now under the New Covenant. The Old Covenant was "old" because it was ratified by the blood of bulls and goats at the time of Moses. The New Covenant is "new" because it was ratified by the blood of our Lord Jesus Christ on the cross of Calvary.[153] Therefore, the New Testament believer—whether Jew or Gentile—is under the New Covenant. The Old Covenant had the earthly sanctuary and its services (Exod. 25:8). The New Covenant believer has the heavenly sanctuary and its services (Heb. 9). All blood sacrifices find their fulfillment in Christ Jesus our Lord and Savior.[154] In Romans 8:34, Paul summarized the gospel as revealed in both the earthly and heavenly sanctuary services: "It is Christ who died, and furthermore is also risen, who is even at the right hand of God, who also makes intercession for us." He is clearly using sanctuary imagery in portraying the way of salvation.

So even now, under the New Covenant, we believe in Jesus as our Sacrifice and our High Priest. We follow Him by faith in the heavenly sanctuary above just as the ancient Israelites followed the high priest by faith when he went into the earthly sanctuary to perform his ministry. Ellen White succinctly summarized the heavenly sanctuary ministry of Christ our Lord.

The incense, ascending with the prayers of Israel, represents the merits and intercession of Christ, His perfect righteousness, which through faith is imputed to His people, and which can alone make the worship of sinful beings

---

[153] *Patriarchs and Prophets*, pp. 370, 371.
[154] *The Seventh-day Adventist Bible Commentary*, vol. 1, p. 694.

acceptable to God. Before the veil of the most holy place, was an altar of perpetual intercession, before the holy, an altar of continual atonement. By blood and by incense, God was to be approached—symbols pointing to the great Mediator, through whom sinners may approach Jehovah, and through whom alone mercy and salvation can be granted to the repentant, believing soul.[155]

The New Testament believer, whether Jew or Gentile, is part of the "Israel of God" (Gal. 6:16; 1 Peter 2:9; Rom. 2:28, 29). As Ellen White observed, all who accept Christ as Savior become the true "Israel of God."[156] Jesus is interceding by His blood in the heavenly sanctuary for all who accept the gospel (Rom. 8:34). "But He, because He continues forever, has an unchangeable priesthood. Therefore He is also able to save to the uttermost those who come to God through Him, since He always lives to make intercession for them" (Heb. 7:24, 25).[157]

---

[155] *The Faith I Live By*, p. 197.

[156] *The Desire of Ages*, p. 288, etc.

[157] See *Amazing Grace*, p. 154, as a wonderful description of Christ's ministry for us.

CHRIST OUR RIGHTEOUSNESS— OUR WONDERFUL JUDGE

Chapter 10

Christ—Our Merciful High Priest

In 1899, Frank E. Belden, Ellen White's nephew, wrote the hymn, "Cover with His Life." This means that more than 100 years ago the grand truth of Christ our righteousness in the hour of God's judgment was set to music. What a blessedness it is to know that our merciful High Priest stands for us in judgment.

> Look upon Jesus, sinless is He;
> Father, impute His life unto me.
> My life of scarlet, my sin and woe,
> Cover with His life, whiter than snow.
> Deep are the wounds transgression has made;
> Red are the stains; my soul is afraid.
> O to be covered, Jesus, with Thee,
> Safe from the law that now judgeth me![158]

Since the judgment is the one theme that God's people should be most familiar with as we approach the second coming of Christ, it is very important that we bring this topic to the forefront as we see the day approaching. Ellen White reminds us: "The subject of the sanctuary and the investigative judgment should be clearly understood by the people of God. All need a knowledge for themselves of the position and work of their great High Priest."[159] Again, we are told, "We need to humble ourselves before

---

[158] Frank E. Belden, "Cover With His Life," *Seventh-day Adventist Hymnal* (1985), hymn no. 412.
[159] *The Great Controversy*, p. 488.

the Lord, with fasting and prayer, and to meditate much upon his Word, especially upon the scenes of the judgment."[160]

Unfortunately, many view judgment with fear and trepidation. Most often, judgment is understood as condemnation and punishment. It is true there can be no condemnation without judgment. However, it is also true there can be no acquittal without judgment (Deut. 25:1). In other words, God cannot declare us innocent in Christ before the universe without a judgment that shows us to be so.

The concept of a final judgment is brought to view in both the Old and the New Testaments. Abraham had confidence in God as the Judge of all the earth (Gen. 18:25). In the New Testament, Jesus is presented as the One who will be the Judge (John 5:22; Heb. 10:30). This means that our Substitute and Surety is also our Wonderful Judge. He is the One who absolutely knows every case, every person's wretchedness and repentance and faith.[161] He takes into consideration the advantages and disadvantages of each. He even considers where and when we were born (Ps. 87:6). He is "not willing that any should perish but that all should come to repentance" (2 Peter 3:9). His heart cry for us is that we turn from our wicked ways, for He has no pleasure in the death of the wicked (Jer. 8:21, 22; Ezek. 18:30–32; 33:11).

> "It is true that there can be no condemnation without judgment. However, it is also true that there can be no acquittal without judgment."

The New Testament clearly states that we must all stand before the judgment seat of Christ (Rom. 14:10; 2 Cor. 5:10). God will judge both the dead and the living according to their works (2 Tim. 4:1; 1 Peter 4:5; Eccl. 3:17; 12:13, 14; 1 Peter 4:17). Alluding to sanctuary imagery, Ellen White plainly indicates what happens in the judgment. "Some men's sins

---

[160] *Review and Herald*, Jan. 10, 1907.
[161] *Testimonies for the Church*, vol. 5, p. 474.

are open beforehand, confessed in penitence, and forsaken, and they go beforehand to judgment. Pardon is written over against the names of these men. But other men's sins follow after, and are not put away by repentance and confession, and these sins will stand registered against them in the books of heaven."[162]

The books of heaven

We have talked about pardon and justification and about sins going "beforehand to judgment" to be blotted out. In the heavenly accounts, there is a record of all our praise, prayers, and confession of sin (Ps. 56:8; 139:16; Mal. 3:16). Everything about us—our thoughts, our feelings, our holy endeavors, and even our slips and falls—are in God's books of remembrance. Our Heavenly Father knows all about us individually. The Psalmist declares:

> Where can I go from Your Spirit?
> Or where can I flee from Your presence?
>
> If I ascend into heaven, You are there;
> If I make my bed in hell [sheōl, the grave],
> Behold, You are there.
>
> If I take the wings of the morning,
> And dwell in the uttermost parts of the sea,
> Even there Your hand shall lead me,
> And Your right hand shall hold me.
>
> If I say, "Surely the darkness shall fall on me,"
> Even the night shall be light about me;

---

[162] *The Seventh-day Adventist Bible Commentary*, vol. 7, p. 916.

Indeed, the darkness shall not hide from You,
But the night shines as the day;
The darkness and the light are both alike to You.
    (Ps. 139:7–12)

Moreover, Jesus tells us that even the hairs of our head are numbered (Matt. 10:30), and the Psalmist says, "He counts the number of the stars; He calls them all by name" (Ps. 147:4; cf. Isa. 40:26). Paul says of Jesus, "All things were created through Him and for Him" (Col. 1:16). The Creator of the universe knows the place and functioning of every particle. Even our thoughts and the intentions of our hearts are open to Him; they are as clear as sunlight (Gen. 6:5; Ps. 139:2). And Paul says, "In Him we live and move and have our being" (Acts 17:28).

Because God is so intimately acquainted with our very being, He counsels us, "Let the wicked forsake his way, and the unrighteous man his thoughts; let him return to the LORD, and He will have mercy on him; and to our God, for He will abundantly pardon" (Isa. 55:7). Paul explains how this is possible through the provisions of the gospel. Through the working of the Holy Spirit in our souls, "bringing every thought into captivity to the obedience of Christ," we live the Christian life in harmony with God's holy will (2 Cor. 10:5).

It is not to jog God's memory that He keeps a record of the names and deeds of each of us for all time. It is for the benefit of the entire universe, so that all may see the justice and mercy of God in His dealing with the sin problem. Both Daniel and John saw that the record books of heaven were the basis of the judgment. Daniel says, "The court was seated, and the books were opened" (Dan. 7:10). John saw, at the great white throne judgment, that "books were opened. And another book was opened, which is the Book of Life. And the dead were judged according to their works, by the things which were written in the books" (Rev. 20:12). This is so because God has promised to "bring every work into judgment, including every secret thing, whether good or evil" (Eccl. 12:14). Then, when Jesus comes, He will say, "My reward is with Me, to give to every one according to his work" (Rev. 22:12). The demonstration of perfect justice requires perfect accounts. On the other hand, perfect mercy also requires perfect records.

Moses was aware of these heavenly records. He prayed that, if God could not forgive Israel, he might be blotted out with them. "Yet now, if You will forgive their sin—but if not, I pray, blot me out of Your book which You have written" (Exod. 32:32). Note that this is a book of God's own writing. "In the prayer of Moses our minds are directed to the heavenly records in which the names of all men are inscribed, and their deeds, whether good or evil, are faithfully registered. The book of life contains the names of all who have ever entered the service of God."[163] In the judgment, Jesus says that the one who "overcomes shall be clothed in white garments, and I will not blot out his name from the Book of Life; but I will confess his name before My Father and before His angels" (Rev. 3:5). Certainly our Advocate would not blot a person's name out of the Book of Life without a fair and open judgment.

So, in the judgment, Jesus is not only our Judge, Substitute, and Surety, but He is also our Advocate in the heavenly sanctuary. The apostle John wrote, "My little children, these things I write to you, so that you may not sin. And if anyone sins, we have an Advocate with the Father, Jesus Christ the righteous. And He Himself is the propitiation for our sins, and not for ours only but also for the whole world" (1 John 2:1, 2). During this judgment, Jesus brings us into "at-onement" with Himself. The dictionary usage of the word "atonement" helps us to relate to it. It was first used in the year 1575 and may have come from "atone + -ment as the translation of the Medieval Latin *adūnāmentum*; however, the noun is found earlier than the verb (*atone*); and in this light, the proper etymology is at + onement."[164] This final "at-onement" in the judgment blots out our sins and seals us into oneness with Christ for eternity, thereby fulfilling Jesus' prayer of John 17. Just as in Old Testament times the judge was on the

---

[163] *Patriarchs and Prophets*, p. 326.
[164] "Atonement," wiktionary, available at http://1ref.us/rp, accessed 2/27/2019.

side of the accused (Deut. 19:17–19; 32:36), so our Wonderful Judge is on our side—He is our Advocate, and He facilitates our oneness with Him.

The work of our heavenly High Priest

When it comes to the judgment, Jesus says that the Father Himself loves us and is not willing that we should be lost. Why then does Jesus advocate for us before the Father? The issue is that God is unchangeable and His law is unchangeable (Mal. 3:6). Moreover, Paul says that the law is "holy and just and good" (Rom. 7:12). The question then follows: How can God be just and the justifier of those who rely upon Jesus for salvation? How can God save sinners whom He loves and still be just before the universe? These are the questions that puzzled Satan's mind and that still puzzle the minds of many today.

In relation to the law

Before we go further, let us look at God's holy law for a moment. The principles of these Ten Commandments are eternal—as eternal as the throne of God. They are universal—encompassing love to God and to all humankind (Matt. 22:37–40). The happiness of the entire universe depends on all of God's creatures living in harmony with His holy law.[165] The prophet Amos spoke for God when he asked, "Can two walk together, unless they are agreed?" (Amos 3:3). God does not change. He is eternally the same (Heb. 13:8). We would not want Him to be otherwise. When anarchy reigns, no one is safe or happy. There is only bedlam. Eternity in an environment like that would be hell.

---

[165] See *Steps to Christ*, p. 62; *The Spirit of Prophecy*, vol. 1, p. 22; *Testimonies for the Church*, vol. 1, p. 132.

It has often been said that God's holy law is a transcript of His character.[166] How could it be anything else? It is unimaginable that God would give a law that would not be in harmony with His thought and person. Indeed, He says, "I am the Lord, I do not change" (Mal. 3:6).

Note the scriptural references that refer to both God and His holy law.

The character of God and His law are the same.		
God's Character	The Essential Attribute	God's Law
Ps. 19:2	Everlasting	Ps. 111:7, 8
Deut. 7:9	Faithful	Ps. 119:86
Matt. 19:17	Good	Rom. 7:12
Lev. 19:2	Holy	Rom. 7:12
Deut. 32:4	Just	Rom. 7:12
1 John 1:2; 5:20	Life	John 12:50
1 John 1:5	Light	Prov. 6:23
1 John 4:8	Love	Rom. 13:10
Isa. 9:6	Peace	Ps. 119:165
Matt. 5:48	Perfect	Ps. 19:7
1 John 3:3	Pure	Ps. 19:8
Ps. 145:17	Righteous	Ps. 119:172; Deut. 4:8
1 Cor. 10:4; John 4:24	Spiritual	Rom. 7:14
John 14:6	Truth	Ps. 119:142
Col. 2:3	Wisdom	Ps. 119:97–99

Although it is in the writings of Paul where we find the majority of the scriptural statements about Christ's imputed righteousness, yet it is also in the writings of Paul that we find a consistent call for sanctified living through obedience to God's holy law. Ellen White commented on Paul's writings on the law:

> Paul dwelt especially upon the far-reaching claims of God's law. He showed how it extends to the deep secrets of man's moral nature and throws a flood of light upon

---

[166] *Christ's Object Lessons*, p. 305.

that which has been concealed from the sight and knowledge of men. What the hands may do or the tongue may utter—what the outer life reveals—but imperfectly shows man's moral character. The law searches his thoughts, motives, and purposes. The dark passions that lie hidden from the sight of men, the jealousy, hatred, lust, and ambition, the evil deeds meditated upon in the dark recesses of the soul, yet never executed for want of opportunity—all these God's law condemns.[167]

The description of this good and perfect law fully aligns with what Jesus was in His humanity when He was on earth (John 15:10). He says, "He who has seen Me has seen the Father" (John 14:9). Our Wonderful Judge is the same yesterday, today, and forever (Heb. 13:8). His righteousness knows no end. It is no wonder that God's holy law of Ten Commandments is the only standard of righteousness in the final judgment (James 2:10–12). He wants to save us in His eternal kingdom where we will be fully in harmony with His eternal principles of righteousness—the principles of love to God and love to one another. Such harmony will be in body, soul, and spirit and in intention, desire, and purpose. In other words, Jesus wants us to be fully in harmony with Him and the Father, without a single inkling or thought of being otherwise. In the words of Ellen White, to be fully in harmony with Jesus means "to be absolutely and completely for Him in this world as He is for us in the presence of God."[168]

Our Wonderful Judge came to earth to do for us what it was impossible for us to do for ourselves. He promises, "The one who comes to Me I will by no means cast out" (John 6:37). He implores: "Come to me, all you who labor and are heavy laden, and I will give you rest" (Matt. 11:28). What other judge has ever said, "I, even I, am He who blots out your transgressions for My own sake; and I will not remember your sins" (Isa. 43:25)?

---

[167] *Acts of the Apostles*, p. 424.
[168] *Acts of the Apostles*, p. 566.

Of Jesus, Peter said: "It is He who was ordained by God to be Judge of the living and the dead" (Acts 10:42). And Jesus said: "For the Father judges no one, but has committed all judgment to the Son" (John 5:22).

In relation to the love of the Father and the Son

Let us consider for a moment this great event taking place in the heavenly sanctuary. There we see the Father of our Lord Jesus Christ, and there we see the Son, who is the Lamb slain from the foundation of the world, interceding as our High Priest and ministering His forgiveness and righteousness for us. We also see the law of Ten Commandments by which we are judged. Encircling this most solemn and majestic scene are the angels and the on-looking universe. All heaven is intently interested in the outcome of the judgment.

It is the love of the Father that made provision for this judgment scene. Jesus said, "I do not say to you that I shall pray the Father for you; *for the Father Himself loves you*" (John 16:26, 27, emphasis added). In this judgment, the "counsel of peace shall be between them both" (Zech. 6:13). That is, the counsel will be between the Father and the Son. Zechariah prophesied that, in the heavenly sanctuary, Christ would be both Priest and King on His Father's throne (see Rev. 3:21). "He shall bear the glory, and shall sit and rule on His [Father's] throne; so He shall be a priest on His throne, and the counsel of peace shall be between them both" (Zech. 6:12, 13).[169] This counsel fulfills the righteous requirement that God Himself set down in Deuteronomy 19:15, "by the mouth of two or three witnesses the matter shall be established."[170] It is the Father and the Son who witness to our innocence before the law of Ten Commandments.

As the counsel of peace is between Them both, that means both the Father and the Son are on our side. God is doing everything possible in

---

[169] See *The Great Controversy*, pp. 415, 416; insertion in Zechariah by the author.
[170] See also Heb. 10:28, 29.

His great and vast universe to assure us that we will be with Him in eternity. Together the Father and the Son judge whether we have, by repentance and faith, accepted Christ's imputed righteousness and cooperated with the Holy Spirit to transform our character to be in harmony with His holy law. Since all are to be judged by "the law of liberty" (James 2:10–12), it is necessary that two witnesses agree that we are innocent. It is the office of the judge, in the face of two or three witnesses, to "justify the righteous and condemn the wicked" (Deut. 25:1). Thus, the Father and the Son, through the "counsel of peace between them both," bear witness that we have cooperated with the great plan of salvation and are accounted worthy of a place in Their eternal kingdom. Ellen White encouragingly states, "All who have truly repented of sin, and by faith claimed the blood of Christ as their atoning sacrifice, have had pardon entered against their names in the books of heaven; as they have become partakers of the righteousness of Christ, and their characters are found to be in harmony with the law of God, their sins will be blotted out, and they themselves will be accounted worthy of eternal life."[171]

Our Wonderful Judge is not trying to keep anyone out of heaven. Rather, He has done and is doing all that it is Godly possible that we might be with Him in eternity. "For God so loved the world that He gave His only begotten Son" and all that it involves "that whoever believes in Him should not perish but have everlasting life" (John 3:16). What more could Jesus do than to die for us the second death, which would mean our eternal separation from our Holy God. We are told that Jesus, while on the cross, could not see beyond the tomb.[172] That is what we would have without Him. Yet, "by faith, Christ was victor."[173] Now He intercedes for us in the heavenly sanctuary His righteousness before the loving Father and His holy law, and He graciously grants us His Holy Spirit so that we may appreciate all that He has done and glorify His holy name by living for Him.

---

[171] *The Great Controversy*, p. 483.
[172] *The Desire of Ages*, p. 753.
[173] *The Desire of Ages*, p. 756.

What more can we do but, with a heart full of love, come to Him in repentance and faith and accept all that He is doing for us? For indeed, it is "by repentance and faith" that "we are enabled to render obedience to all of the commandments of God, and to be found without blame before Him."[174]

Cooperating with our Wonderful High Priest

As we noted in SECTION THREE, in the earthly sanctuary service, the believer followed the high priest in his priestly rituals on the Day of Atonement by faith alone. He gathered with others to the sanctuary, but he did not go into the sanctuary. Only by faith could he follow his representative, the high priest, as he went into the Most Holy Place in the presence of God. The rituals on the Day of Atonement in ancient Israel cleansed the people and the sanctuary and removed the record of sin far from them—indeed as far as the east is from the west (Lev. 16; Ps. 103:12).

> "*The believer followed the high priest in his priestly rituals on the Day of Atonement by faith alone.*"

Both the Old Testament and the New must be viewed in the light of God's dealing with sin through the sanctuary ceremonies. The Psalmist said that His way "is in the sanctuary" (Ps. 77:13). The New Testament writers were very familiar with the earthly temple. Their mindset of the way of salvation was that salvation is in the sanctuary. The Holy Spirit spoke to and through them, testifying that Jesus' sacrifice and ministry in the heavenly sanctuary are the antitype of the earthly sanctuary rituals (Hebrews 8–10). The early church was of Jewish origin and culture.

---

[174] *Testimonies for the Church*, vol. 5, p. 472; compare Acts 20:21; "Now, while our great High Priest is making the atonement for us, we should seek to become perfect in Christ" (*The Great Controversy*, p. 623).

In reading the New Testament, we must wear "sanctuary glasses." The church of the New Testament is the continuation of the Israel of God, and it will go through to the end.

Knowing these things, we must direct our attention to the pre-advent judgment in the light of sanctuary imagery. Because the pre-advent judgment of all who have professed the name of Jesus began in 1844 and closes with the living, we need to look at what the final application of the atonement means for us who are living today.[175] The overall purpose of the final atonement is to bring us into harmony with the character of Christ so that He may come and take us home to heaven.[176]

It is encouraging to see that this subject has been receiving more attention over the past few years than previously. The investigative judgment is succinctly summarized in the twenty-fourth of the twenty-eight fundamental beliefs of the Seventh-day Adventist Church.[177] This belief reads, in part: "The investigative judgment reveals to heavenly intelligences who among the dead are asleep in Christ and therefore, in Him, are deemed worthy to have part in the first resurrection. It also makes manifest who among the living are abiding in Christ, keeping the commandments of God and the faith of Jesus, and in Him, therefore, are ready for translation into His everlasting kingdom."[178]

> "*Only by faith could he follow his representative, the high priest, as he went into the Most Holy Place in the presence of God.*"

However, there are some searching questions that will need to be answered in the judgment. Jesus "will inquire, What have you done to advance my cause with the talents I lent you? What have you done for me in the person of the poor, the afflicted, the orphan, and the fatherless?

---

[175] For validation of the date, see Clifford Goldstein, *1844 Made Simple* (1988).
[176] *Christ's Object Lessons*, p. 69.
[177] "28 Fundamental Beliefs," available at http://1ref.us/rq, accessed 2/27/2019.
[178] See also *Seventh-day Adventists Believe*, second edition, pp. 347, 348.

I was sick, poor, hungry, and destitute of clothing; what did you do for me with my entrusted means? How was the time I lent you employed? How did you use your pen, your voice, your money, your influence? I made you the depositary of a precious trust by opening before you the thrilling truths heralding my second coming. What have you done with the light and knowledge I gave you to make men wise unto salvation?"[179]

Our only fitting response, through the prompting of the indwelling Spirit, is to yield to conviction and follow His example in ministry to the underserved. As Paul says, "For by grace you have been saved through faith, and that not of yourselves; it is the gift of God, not of works, lest anyone should boast"; the result being that "we are His workmanship, created in Christ Jesus for good works, which God prepared beforehand that we should walk in them" (Eph. 2:8–10). The good works that God has foreordained, which we live in, are to bring glory to God in the judgment (Matt. 5:16 and Rev. 14:7).

Of our day, Ellen White wrote, "We are in the great day of atonement, when our sins are, by confession and repentance, to go beforehand to judgment. God does not now accept a tame, spiritless testimony from His ministers. Such a testimony would not be present truth. The message for this time must be meat in due season to feed the church of God. But Satan has been seeking gradually to rob this message of its power that the people may not be prepared to stand in the day of the Lord."[180]

Conclusion

As we have seen, the final atonement is committed to Jesus our Substitute and Surety. He now is our Wonderful Judge and Advocate. In the New Covenant, as the believers did in the Old, we follow by faith our great High Priest and Judge as He ministers for us in the Most Holy Place of

---

[179] *Signs of the Times*, Nov. 20, 1884; see also Matt. 25:31–40.

[180] *Selected Messages*, book 1, p. 124.

the heavenly sanctuary.[181] "It is those who by faith follow Jesus in the great work of the atonement who receive the benefits of His mediation in their behalf."[182] As it was with the believing Israelite so it is with us. Since we are living in the antitypical Day of Atonement, our sins are to go before-hand to judgment (1 Tim. 5:24, KJV) so they may be blotted out when the times of refreshing come from the presence of the Lord; and He sends us Jesus Christ (Acts 3:19, 20).[183]

It is given to us to cooperate with Jesus as He ministers in our behalf to remove sin from us and, ultimately, from the universe. It is by repentance and faith that we are cleansed from all sin (1 John 1:7–9) and our sins are blotted out in the judgment (1 Tim. 5:24, KJV; Acts 3:19). When our sins are blotted out of the records of heaven, Jesus can show before the universe that "the life of His trusting disciples would be like His, a series of uninterrupted victories, not seen to be such here, but recognized as such in the great hereafter."[184]

Walking in the light that streams from the heavenly sanctuary, we may come to God's throne of grace and be covered for eternity with Christ's imputed righteousness. In the "closing up of the great day of atonement," Christ asks for us "not only pardon and justification, full and complete, but a share in His glory and a seat upon His throne."[185]

---

[181] *The Great Controversy*, pp. 424, 425.
[182] *The Great Controversy*, p. 430.
[183] *The Great Controversy*, p. 485.
[184] *The Desire of Ages*, p. 679.
[185] *Testimonies for the Church*, vol. 5, p. 472; *The Great Controversy*, p. 483.

Chapter 11

The Removal of Sin

Sin cannot and will not enter heaven again (Gal. 5:16–21; Nah. 1:9). The heavenly angels will have seen the results of the rebellion Lucifer started in heaven. "The whole universe will have become witnesses to the nature and results of sin..... Never will evil again be manifest..... A tested and proved creation will never again be turned from allegiance to Him whose character has been fully manifested before them as fathomless love and infinite wisdom."[186]

God has made every provision to cleanse us from all sin so that we can enter His eternal presence at the coming of Jesus, unashamed and without fault. Flesh and blood will not inherit the kingdom of God (1 Cor. 15:50). All sin must be dealt with before the coming of Christ. "A character formed according to the divine likeness is the only treasure that we can take from this world to the next;" "and the thoughts and feelings combined make up the moral character."[187] Just as all sin was dealt with on the Day of Atonement in ancient Israel, and sin was blotted out and removed from the earthly sanctuary and the congregation (Lev. 16), so is sin blotted out in the antitypical Day of Atonement. All sin that is sent beforehand by repentance and confession to judgment in the heavenly sanctuary is blotted out. Then will be fully realized the blessing of the New Covenant, "For I will be merciful to their unrighteousness, and their sins and their lawless deeds I will remember no more" (Heb. 8:12).

---

[186] *The Great Controversy*, p. 504.
[187] *Christ's Object Lessons*, p. 332; *Testimonies for the Church*, vol. 5, p. 310.

Cooperation by confession and repentance

The cleansing of the heavenly sanctuary for the removal of the record of sin began in 1844 with all who died in the hope of eternal life.[188] By the very nature of things, that cleansing will end with the judgment for the living. In this final atonement, our Savior wants to judge us innocent and blot out sin from our lives and from the record books of heaven.

The ancient Israelites were to gather to the sanctuary and afflict their souls (Lev. 16:29–31).[189] To afflict the soul means humbling one's self before God with heart searching and repentance and, by repentance and faith, putting away every known sin. Their faith was wholly in the blood of the sacrifice and the ministry of the high priest. It is no different for us today. By repentance and faith, we too are to send our sins on "beforehand ... to judgment" (1 Tim. 5:24, KJV) that they may be blotted out when the "times of refreshing" may be poured out in latter rain power from the presence of the Lord (Acts 3:19).[190]

At present, the most important text we can commit to memory is 1 John 1:9; "If we confess our sins, He is faithful and just to *forgive* us our sins and to *cleanse* us from all unrighteousness" (emphasis added). In repentance, "the heart must be yielded to God—must be subdued by divine grace—before man's repentance can be accepted."[191] This kind of repentance is a pure gift from God (Acts 5:31). "Christ pardons none but the penitent, but whom He pardons He first makes penitent. The provision made is complete, and the eternal righteousness of Christ is placed to the account of every believing soul."[192] "Repentance toward God and faith in our Lord Jesus Christ" were the core and essence of the Apostle Paul's message (Acts 20:20, 21). Indeed, Ellen White gives us the assurance that

---

[188] *Early Writings*, p. 253; *The Great Controversy*, p. 435.

[189] *The Great Controversy*, p. 490.

[190] *The Seventh-day Adventist Bible Commentary*, vol. 7, p. 916; *The Great Controversy*, p. 485.

[191] *Patriarchs and Prophets*, p. 587. See Psalm 51 as a perfect example of repentance.

[192] *A New Life*, p. 23.

by "repentance and faith we are enabled to render obedience to all the commandments of God, and are found without blame before Him."[193]

It is through repentance and faith that we are to "cleanse ourselves from all filthiness of the flesh and spirit, perfecting holiness in the fear of God" (2 Cor. 7:1).[194] It is through repentance and faith that our "sins are open beforehand, going before to judgment" to be dealt with in the great Antitypical Day of Atonement (1 Tim. 5:24, KJV).[195] Repentance "is the only process by which infinite purity reflects the image of Christ in His redeemed subjects."[196] And, in every aspect of the pre-advent judgment we are to constantly remember that it is our blessed Lord through the Holy Spirit that brings this blessing of repentance to us (Acts 5:31, 32; John 16:7, 8). Indeed, as we open our hearts to receive the Holy Spirit through Christ our Savior, the Holy Spirit brings every other blessing in His train.[197]

Coming to the judgment as sinners

One of the most impressive narratives depicting the "closing up" of the great Day of Atonement is the vision of Zechariah 3, regarding Joshua and the Angel. Ellen White tells us, "Zechariah's vision of Joshua and the Angel applies with peculiar force to the experience of God's people in the closing up of the great day of atonement."[198] The great day of the final atonement closes with the judgment of the living. Joshua, as a representative of God's people, is standing before the Lord in filthy garments with nothing to say in his own defense. It is the Lord who takes up his case and answers the charges of Satan, the enemy.

---

[193] *Testimonies for the Church*, vol. 5, p. 472.

[194] The concepts of repentance and faith are found in verses 9 and 10.

[195] *The Great Controversy*, p. 620.

[196] *The Seventh-day Adventist Bible Commentary*, vol. 7, p. 1068.

[197] *The Desire of Ages*, p. 672.

[198] *Testimonies for the Church*, vol. 5, p. 472.

In the natural course of things, the judgment must pass from the cases of the dead to the cases of the living. Zechariah's vision represents Joshua as coming to the judgment in filthy garments, confessing himself a sinner. In like manner do we come to the judgment as sinners in need of God's saving grace. It has been asserted in times past that we must be perfectly sinless before we come to the judgment. Zechariah's vision does not indicate this to be the case. Joshua stands in the judgment in "filthy garments" (Zech. 3:3). The filthy garments represent our sinfulness, for "all our righteousnesses are like filthy rags" (Isa. 64:6). Commenting on Zechariah 3, Ellen White succinctly states that the filthy garments of our sinfulness are removed as we "confess and forsake our sins, that they may go beforehand to judgment and be blotted out."[199]

As we come to the judgment, how encouraging are these words: "The filthy garments are removed; for Christ says, 'I have caused thine iniquity to pass from thee.' The iniquity is transferred to the innocent, the pure, the holy Son of God; and man, all undeserving, stands before the Lord cleansed from all unrighteousness, and clothed with the imputed righteousness of Christ. Oh, what a change of raiment is this!"[200] As we, like Joshua of old, stand before our Judge praying in penitence and faith, Jesus "holds before the Father the censer of His own merits, in which there is no taint of earthly corruption. He gathers into this censer the prayers, the praise, and the confessions of His people, and with these He puts His own spotless righteousness. *Then, perfumed with the merits of Christ's propitiation, the incense comes up before God wholly and entirely acceptable.* Then gracious answers are returned."[201]

How important it is that we follow our Wonderful Judge and High Priest by faith and keep pace with the work He is doing for us in the heavenly sanctuary. This is the message for our time because it applies to the closing up of the great Day of Atonement.[202] It needs to be proclaimed

---

[199] *The Seventh-day Adventist Bible Commentary,* vol. 4, p. 1178.
[200] *The Seventh-day Adventist Bible Commentary,* vol. 4, p. 1178.
[201] *Selected Messages,* book 1, p. 344, emphasis added.
[202] *Testimonies for the Church,* vol. 5, p. 472.

from every pulpit and published time and again in Adventism so that our people may not only cooperate with Jesus in the heavenly sanctuary but be prepared to meet Jesus in peace when He comes in the clouds of glory.

The vision of Joshua and the Angel of Zechariah 3 is a message of "present truth" for us today. The Adventist pioneers understood the final atonement to be a process. Ellen White referred to it as a "settling into the truth."[203] My heart thrills at the glory of God when I think of it. Now, even now, by repentance and faith (Acts 20:20, 21; 1 John 1:9), we are to send all our sins on beforehand to judgment that they may be blotted out when the perfecting latter rain, the times of refreshing, shall come from the presence of the Lord.[204]

To show us the significance of cooperating with Him in the final atonement, Jesus gave us the parable of the wedding garment found in Matthew 22. The king provided the garment.[205] The guests were expected to cooperate with the king's gracious offer and wear it. Yet, one guest, in the parable, is found wearing his own clothing. What an insult to the king to come to the wedding without the costly garment the king provided for each guest! Is it any wonder that the guest who refused to wear it was cast out? All heaven is astir in soliciting our cooperation with Christ so that we will not be found without the garment of His righteousness at His second advent.

The blotting out of sin

As stated earlier, the metaphors of removing sin as far as the east is from the west and of casting all our sins into the depths of the sea are in reference to how completely the scapegoat on the Day of Atonement removed the record of sin from the camp of Israel (Ps. 103:12; Micah 7:19; Lev. 16). Sins were not figuratively cast "into the depths of the sea" until after being

---

[203] *The Faith I Live By*, p. 287; see Paul A. Gordon, *The Sanctuary, 1844 and the Pioneers* (2000), p. 146.

[204] *The Faith I Live By*, p. 334; *The Great Controversy*, p. 485.

[205] Christ's Object Lessons, p. 309.

judged and blotted out on the Day of Atonement. There was no other way for God to deal with the sins of His people than through the sanctuary rituals of the sacrificial system in the Old Testament. Under the New Testament, there is "no other name under heaven given among men by which we must be saved" (Acts 4:12), for Jesus is the reality of the sacrificial lamb to take away the sin of the world (John 1:29).

Some have said that, if we are ready for the second coming, we will be ready for the judgment. They use Ellen White's statement, "If you are right with God today, you are ready if Jesus should come today."[206] Since we know that there are certain things that must transpire before Jesus returns in the clouds of glory, in what way would Jesus come today for you and me? There can be only one way, and that is if we die today.[207] Considering Jesus' coming in the clouds of glory, I would ask, Have we yet received the perfecting latter rain?[208] Have we passed through the seven last plagues and the time of trouble? Do we reflect the image of Jesus fully, as *The Great Controversy* says we will do under the sixth plague?[209] There is a difference between being ready to die in Christ and being ready to meet Him alive in glory when He comes again. There are events our Lord wants to bring us through successfully so that we *will* be ready to meet Him in peace when He comes. This does not mean that our Lord delays His coming. For us, it could be only a heartbeat away.

Now, consider what has been revealed to us about reflecting the image of Jesus fully and about being ready to meet Him in peace at the Second Coming. A few years back, church leaders used *Christ's Object Lessons*, page 69, to "encourage" Seventh-day Adventists to be ready for Jesus when He comes. The statement says, "When the character of Jesus shall be perfectly reproduced in His people, then He will come and claim them as his own." In my ministry, this "encouragement" discouraged many of my people. They knew and I knew that perfect reproduction was not

---

[206] *In Heavenly Places*, p. 227.
[207] *Adult Sabbath School Bible Study Guide*, 4th Quarter 2017, lesson for Thursday, Dec. 21.
[208] *Testimonies for Ministers*, p. 508.
[209] *The Great Controversy*, p. 621.

a reality in our lives. We were all too conscious of the sinfulness of our being. I then did a search of Ellen White's writings on reflecting the image of Jesus fully. I found several statements in which the phrase is used. The following statement is crucial to our understanding: "Repentance for sin is the first fruits of the working of the Holy Spirit in the life. It is the *only process* by which infinite purity reflects the image of Christ in His redeemed subjects (emphasis added)."[210] What impressed me most, however, was a statement that reveals that even up to the sixth plague, after probation has closed, we obviously still do not reflect the image of Jesus *fully*. We are told that the fiery furnace of the seven last plagues—especially the sixth plague—is necessary for our "earthliness" to "be consumed, that the image of Christ may be perfectly reflected."[211] It would appear that even up to the sixth plague there is still more to be done in us that we might reflect the image of Jesus fully. Through all this, we are in our Savior's hands. In Him "we are more than conquerors through Him who loved us" (Rom. 8:37). Certainly, in comparing *Christ's Object Lessons*, page 69, with *The Great Controversy*, page 621, we learn that Jesus will come and take us home to heaven when we reflect His image fully.

In contemplating perfect reproduction of the image of Jesus, it is essential that we remember Jesus' parable about the growth of the seed— first the blade, then the ear, and then the full corn in the ear. At every stage the plant is perfect—perfect in its formation—according to its intended design (Mark 4:28, 29).[212] So it can be with us. As we grow in the grace and knowledge of our Lord Jesus Christ (2 Peter 3:18), exemplifying both the active and passive virtues of the Christian life, we are reflecting the character of our blessed Lord.[213] In that reflection, we may be perfect

---

[210] Ms. 28, 1905.

[211] *The Great Controversy*, p. 621.

[212] *Christ's Object Lessons*, p. 65.

[213] "The active virtues must be cultivated as well as the passive. The Christian, while he is ever ready to give the soft answer that turneth away wrath, must possess the courage of a hero to resist evil. With the charity that endureth all things, he must have the force of character which will make his influence a positive power for good. Faith must be wrought into his character. His principles must be firm; he must be noble-spirited, above all suspicion of meanness" (*Colporteur Ministry*, p. 62).

because our sins are perfectly forgiven.[214] The perfection Jesus is asking of us at this time is that we be as perfectly for Him in this life as He is for us in the heavenly sanctuary.[215] Moreover, we may rest in the promise of God that He "has made provision that we may become like unto Him, and He will accomplish this for all who do not interpose a perverse will and thus frustrate His grace."[216]

I cannot emphasize often enough how important it is for us to cooperate with our Wonderful Judge and High Priest as He ministers for us in the heavenly sanctuary. In the judgment, the cooperation needed is that we be sensitive to the Holy Spirit's work in our lives as He reveals our sins to us. Then, by repentance and confession of our sins, we accept by faith the ministration of Christ's righteousness for us in the heavenly sanctuary. This heart-felt relationship with Christ is the means by which we send all our sins beforehand to judgment to be blotted out of the record books of heaven when the times of refreshing—the perfecting latter rain—come from the presence of our Lord and Savior. And, not only are our sins blotted out in heaven, but Jesus has promised "to cleanse us from all unrighteousness" (1 John 1:9).

Cooperating with Jesus from start to finish

The early and the latter rain are metaphors used in Scripture to represent the outpouring of the Holy Spirit—first at Pentecost (the early rain) and then just before Jesus returns (the latter rain). This is why there is such intense interest in the work of the Holy Spirit in the Seventh-day Adventist Church at this time. In the 1960s there were many compilations from the writings of Ellen White outlining last-day events. Some of these compilations were put together by leaders of the church, but many more were the work of church members, who simply wanted to get the word out to

---

[214] *Selected Messages*, vol. 2, p. 32.
[215] *Acts of the Apostles*, p. 566.
[216] *Amazing Grace*, p. 134.

prepare for the final events of this earth's history. A number of these compilations were quite elaborate with extensive charts. Almost all of them were based on behavioral perfectionism—the idea that sinless perfection is required to enter the judgment and receive the latter rain. It became obvious that a correct understanding of these things and our relation to them is crucial if we are to cooperate with Christ in this closing work.

The final phase of the atonement and the latter rain are closely connected. Acts 3:19–21 is set in an eschatological, or end-time, framework. The passage talks of repentance, conversion, removal of sin, and the second coming of Jesus. This is sanctuary imagery, for in the sanctuary service of old, sins were removed—blotted out—when the scapegoat symbolically bore them into the wilderness (Lev. 16:21; Isa. 43:25; 44:22), thus effacing their record.[217]

In the chapter in *The Great Controversy* entitled, "The Investigative Judgment," there are many precious thoughts that will guide us in the understanding of the necessity of having a judgment before sins are finally blotted out. We are told, "Beginning with those who first lived upon the earth, our Advocate presents the cases of each successive generation, and closes with the living."[218] We are also told, "The work of the investigative judgment and the blotting out of sins is to be accomplished before the second advent of the Lord.… It is impossible that the sins of men should be blotted out until after the judgment at which their cases are to be investigated. But the apostle Peter distinctly states that the sins of believers will be blotted out 'when the times of refreshing shall come from the presence of the Lord; and He shall send Jesus Christ.'"[219]

Jesus is our Advocate *and* our Wonderful Judge. He presents our cases, not only before the Father but also before the universe. As on the Day of Atonement in the sanctuary of old, the high priest symbolically bore the names of Israel upon his heart into the Most Holy Place (Exod. 28:30), so in the heavenly sanctuary, in the latter days, Christ bears our

---

[217] *Signs of the Times*, May 16, 1895.

[218] *The Great Controversy*, p. 483.

[219] *The Great Controversy*, p. 485, quoting from Acts 3:19, 20, KJV.

names upon His great heart of love and upon the palms of His hands (Isa. 49:16). The purpose of the final atonement is to cleanse us from our sins that we may be at one with Jesus and that we may be prepared to live in the sight of a holy God without a mediator during the seven last plagues.[220] In the time of the judgment of the living, the New Covenant finds its complete fulfillment—"For I will be merciful to their unrighteousness, and their sins and their lawless deeds I will remember no more" (Heb. 8:12).[221]

The judgment of the living as a thief in the night

One summer I was asked to be the speaker at a layman's camp meeting in Castor, Alberta. In the presentation that I gave, I mentioned, on the basis of *The Great Controversy*, page 490, that the judgment of the living comes to God's church as a thief-in-the-night experience. I also pointed out that Revelation 3:3–5, which is quoted in this passage, is couched in Day of Atonement sanctuary imagery. It speaks of repentance and of judgment and sins blotted out. Christ our High Priest confesses before the Father and the holy angels the names of those who have overcome (Luke 12:8, 9; Rev. 3:5).

At the end of my presentation, the conference president, who was in attendance, came to me and asked how I had come to the conclusion that the judgment of the living would come to the church as a thief. I turned to the passage, and we read it together. "The judgment is now passing in the sanctuary above. For many years this work has been in progress. Soon— none know how soon—it will pass to the cases of the living.... At this time above all others it behooves every soul to heed the Saviour's admonition: ... 'If therefore thou shalt not watch, I will come on thee as a thief, and thou shalt not know what hour I will come upon thee.' Revelation 3:3."[222] "Well," he said, "I guess you can't deny that."

---

[220] *Early Writings*, p. 71.
[221] See also *Prophets and Kings*, p. 592.
[222] *The Great Controversy*, pp. 490, 491.

On the basis of this passage, it seems clear that the judgment of the living is a thief-in-the-night experience for God's church. It is in this experience that the separation takes place, when one is taken and the other left (Luke 17:34–36).[223] One group receives the seal of God, and the other receives the mark of the beast. Then probation closes.[224] When probation closes, and the seven last plagues begin falling upon the earth, God's people, having been sealed in the judgment, will then be covered and protected by Christ's imputed righteousness (Isa. 26:20, 21).[225] Thus we are enabled to stand in the sight of a holy God without a mediator.

Christ's return in the clouds of glory will not be as a thief to the saved. Paul says, "But you, brethren, are not in darkness, so that this Day should overtake you as a thief" (1 Thess. 5:4). With a death decree having been legislated and put into effect about the time of the third plague (Rev. 13:15; 16:4–6), the saved and unsaved will not be working side by side in the field when Jesus returns (Matt. 24:40, 41). Besides, God's people will know that Christ is about to arrive because God Himself will announce the day and the hour of Christ's return.[226] These two facts alone tell us that Christ's return in glory will not be as a thief to His people.

Needless to say, a balanced concept of the judgment of the living needs to be proclaimed among God's last-day people. I am deeply concerned whenever people use John 5:24 to preach that there is no judgment for believers. Granted, this passage may be translated, "shall not come into judgment." However, such a rendering contradicts Paul's statements in Romans 14:10 and 2 Corinthians 5:10, where Paul clearly says that "we"— which includes himself—shall all appear "before the judgment seat of Christ." And Paul himself was looking forward to the verdict of Christ,

---

[223] *Testimonies for Ministers*, pp. 234, 235; see also Matthew 24:37–44.

[224] *The Great Controversy*, pp. 490–491.

[225] "The Lord Jesus Christ has prepared a covering, the robe of his own righteousness, that he will put on every repenting, believing soul who by faith will receive it." Review and Herald, November 15, 1898 p. 2. (See also Early Writings p. 43.)

[226] *The Great Controversy*, p. 640.

saying, "There is laid up for me the crown of righteousness, which the Lord, the righteous Judge, will give to me on that Day" (2 Tim. 4:8).

Therefore, John 5:24 is best translated as it is in the KJV and other versions—"shall not come into *condemnation*" as the result of judgment. That this is a valid translation is seen in the fact that even the NIV, which translates the word in John 5:24 as "be judged," translates the same word as "be condemned" in James 5:12. *A Greek-English Lexicon of the New Testament* states that the word *krisis* often means a judgment that goes against a person and, in such a case, the word is translated "condemnation" or "punishment."[227] When John 5:24 states that the believer does not come into condemnation and Romans 14:10 and 2 Corinthians 5:10 clearly state that we shall "all stand/appear before the judgment seat of Christ," we must follow sound principles of translation to not make the Bible contradict itself. It is unwise to translate the Bible to make one portion contradict another when the passage can legitimately be translated to be in harmony with the rest of the Bible.

A "falling away"

Concerning the scriptural teaching of a pre-advent judgment, which takes place in heaven, God has informed us that some will draw back from this foundational doctrine of the Seventh-day Adventist Church. Shortly after 1844, God revealed to Ellen White that this would happen. A reference in *Early Writings*, quoted in *Ellen G. White and Her Critics* by F. D. Nichol, shows that some who formerly believed the sanctuary message would abandon it. I will quote Ellen White's statement at length so the essence of the scene that she saw in vision may be understood.

> I saw a throne, and on it sat the Father and the Son.... I
> saw the Father rise from the throne, ... and in a flaming

---

[227] Bauer, Arndt, and Gingrich, *A Greek-English Lexicon of the New Testament* (1957), p. 453.

chariot go into the holy of holies within the veil, and sit down. Then Jesus rose up from the throne, and the most of those who were bowed down arose with Him.... Those who rose up with Jesus would send up their faith to Him in the holiest, and pray, "My Father, give us Thy Spirit." Then Jesus would breathe upon them the Holy Ghost. In that breath was light, power, and much love, joy, and peace.

I turned to look at the company who were still bowed before the throne; they did not know that Jesus had left it. Satan *appeared* to be by the throne, trying to carry on the work of God. I saw them look up to the throne, and pray, "Father, give us Thy Spirit." Satan would then breathe upon them an unholy influence ... Satan's object was to keep them deceived and to draw back and deceive God's children.[228]

This is where the quotation ends in *Early Writings*. However, that is not the end of what she originally had to say. F. D. Nichol, in his book *Ellen G. White and Her Critics*, explains that the last part of the paragraph was edited out because it was considered redundant. The original paragraph ended with the statement: "I saw one after another leave the company who were praying to Jesus in the Holiest, and go and join those before the throne, and they at once received the unholy influence of Satan."[229]

It is unfortunate that the central doctrine of the Seventh-day Adventist Church—the sanctuary doctrine—has been rejected by some and neglected by others. Yet, currently our leaders in the conferences and divisions are doing much to bring this wonderfully assuring doctrine to the attention of our people. Besides several other publications, I can speak

---

[228] *Early Writings,* pp. 54–56, emphasis added. This representation does not place Satan actually in heaven.

[229] Francis D. Nichol, *Ellen G. White and Her Critics*, p. 624. For the original wording, see *The Day-Star*, March 14, 1846, and "To the Little Flock Scattered Abroad," April 6, 1846.

specifically of the fourth quarter *Sabbath School Quarterly* of 2013, and the second quarter *Sabbath School Quarterly* of 2018. Although a significant number of our members do not attend Sabbath School, I believe this will have its effect and bring our present condition to the forefront.

Moreover, this is the basic reason why I am sharing this topic with you in this little book—so that your confidence may be strong in God's Word and in the gift of prophecy through Ellen White, and so that you can have the greatest hope by cooperating with our Wonderful Judge in the judgment of the living. We are now in the Day of Atonement for the living—the day of "at-onement" with our blessed Lord. Knowing that I am guilty yet will be declared innocent in the judgment, would I not want to rush to the judgment in cooperating with my Wonderful Judge by sending all my sins on beforehand to judgment to be forgiven, to be cleansed, to have my sins blotted out, and to be sealed with the seal of the living God for eternity, nevermore to leave the God I love?

God has made the Seventh-day Adventist Church the depository of His truth for this time—the truth about the pre-advent judgment and the blotting out of sin.[230] Satan knows this better than we do. If it were possible, he would so arrange things as to deceive the very elect. The greatest threats we face in these perilous times are not terrorism and war but the deceptions in the religious world that look so much like New Testament Christianity.

---

[230] *Signs of the Times*, June 1, 1891; Letter 38, 1890, Feb. 21, 1890.

CHRIST OUR RIGHTEOUSNESS IN PERILOUS TIMES

Chapter 12

Perilous Times to Deceive the Elect?

We may be sure perilous times not only await us but are indeed here in the time of God's final atonement for the living. Not only are there lords many and gods many, but the fast pace of life we are now living leaves no room for reflection on the signs of the times thickening around us, which point to the soon return of Jesus. Regarding our day, the physician Luke records Christ's words: "But take heed to yourselves, lest your hearts be weighed down with carousing, drunkenness, and cares of this life, and that Day come on you unexpectedly. For it will come as a snare on all those who dwell on the face of the whole earth. Watch therefore, and pray always that you may be counted worthy to escape all these things that will come to pass, and to stand before the Son of Man" (Luke 21:34–36). If we are watching, we may rest in God's promise, "Surely the Lord GOD does nothing, unless He reveals His secret to His servants the prophets" (Amos 3:7).

A false revival

One of the most perilous deceptions in the last days of earth's history is that "false christs and false prophets will rise and show great signs and wonders to deceive, if possible, even the elect" (Matt. 24:24). Both the Bible and the Spirit of Prophecy emphasize "signs and wonders" as the phenomena in the last days that Satan will employ to deceive the elect of God. Regarding Satan's efforts, Ellen White recorded, "In those churches which he can bring under his deceptive power he will make it appear that

God's special blessing is poured out; there will be manifest what is thought to be great religious interest. Multitudes will exult that God is working marvellously for them, when the work is that of another spirit. Under a religious guise, Satan will seek to extend his influence over the Christian world."[231] Yet, we have no doubt that God is in charge and He has honest children in all denominations.

It is not to disparage any individual seeking to follow the Lord that I present this chapter. God has His honest-hearted children in all persuasions of faith. In the final events that climax earth's history, under the true latter rain of the Holy Spirit, those who are seeking truth will hear and gladly obey present truth for this time (Rev. 18:1–5; 14:6–12).

True and false revivals will both be manifested in these last days. Concerning the latter rain, Ellen White says, "By thousands of voices, all over the earth, the warning will be given. Miracles will be wrought, the sick will be healed, and signs and wonders will follow the believers. Satan also works, with lying wonders, even bringing down fire from heaven in the sight of men. Revelation 13:13. Thus the inhabitants of the earth will be brought to take their stand."[232] Those who are part of the true revival depend entirely on the righteousness of Christ ministered in their behalf in the heavenly sanctuary. Satan's ministers depend on spiritual manifestations for their acceptance with God. They will say in the judgment, "Lord, Lord, have we not prophesied in Your name, cast out demons in Your name, and done many wonders in Your name?" (Matt. 7:22).

The Holy Spirit is given so that we may understand these spiritual things and know truth from error. Solomon wrote, "I will pour out my Spirit on you; I will make known my words to you" (Prov. 1:23). The parallel meaning is clear, for the dissemination of God's words is what happened on the day of Pentecost. Everyone heard the gospel in his or her own dialect (Acts 2:6). This will happen again under the latter rain. However, Satan works to oppose the true outpouring of the Spirit of God.

[231] *The Great Controversy*, p. 464.
[232] *The Great Controversy*, p. 612.

Revelation 13:13 says the false revival will use "great signs, so that he even makes fire come down from heaven on the earth in the sight of men." John the Baptist said Jesus would baptize His people with the "Holy Spirit and fire" (Matt. 3:11). This happened on the day of Pentecost. But Revelation 13:13 tells of a last-day Spirit movement that is to be an overwhelming deception.

The contrast between true and false revivals will be recognized only through the Word of God. In looking down to our time, Ellen White wrote, "This Word is to be our defense when Satan works with such lying wonders that if it were possible he would deceive the very elect. It is then that those who have not stood firmly for the truth will unite with the unbelieving who love and make a lie. When these wonders are performed, when the sick are healed and other marvels are wrought, they will be deceived."[233]

Furthermore, Satan "comes as an angel of light and spreads his influence over the land by means of false reformations. The churches are elated, and consider that God is working marvelously for them, when it is the work of another spirit."[234] In the same passage, Ellen White went on to say of Satan, "Before the loud cry of the third angel is given, he raises an excitement in these religious bodies, that those who have rejected the truth may think that God is with them. He hopes to deceive the honest ... But the light will shine, and all who are honest will ... take their stand with the remnant."[235] Indeed, there are even now signs and wonders intended to deceive God's elect. During the final atonement, "these works of apparent healing will bring Seventh-day Adventists to the test."[236]

In the 1960s, "tongues" and "gifts of the Spirit" crossed all denominational barriers. This "Pentecostal" phenomenon sparked the charismatic

---

[233] *Educational Messenger*, Sept. 11, 1908.

[234] *Early Writings*, p. 260; see also 2 Corinthians 11:14.

[235] *Early Writings*, p. 261; see also *The Great Controversy*, pp. 588, 589. The "loud cry" is a term used to summarize the work of the mighty angel of Revelation 18:1–5. This message repeats the messages of Revelation 14:6–12 when the time comes for them to be given in opposition to the mark of the beast in Revelation 13.

[236] *Selected Messages*, vol. 2, p. 53.

movement and became the greatest force in the ecumenical movement.[237] From that time on, it has morphed into what is now termed "the Third Force,"[238] and this new ecumenism, through the "baptism of the Spirit," is considered the work of the latter rain.[239] It claims to be full gospel, New Testament Christianity, and it calls for abstinence from tobacco, alcohol, drugs, and, until recently, from attendance at movie theaters.[240] These perilous times have the power to deceive because the phenomenon looks and acts so "New Testament." There is good news, however, for, if the counterfeit is here, the true cannot be far behind. Note this counsel: "It is Satan's object now to get up new theories to divert the mind from the true work and genuine message for this time. He stirs up minds to give false interpretation of Scripture, *a spurious loud cry*, that the real message may not have its effect when it does come. *This is one of the greatest evidences that the loud cry will soon be heard and the earth will be lightened with the glory of God.*"[241]

Trying the spirits

The modern method of Biblical interpretation used by dispensationalists prepared the way for a three-fold ecumenical movement. Although forms of dispensationalism have been referenced in various ancient church writings, its modern-day theological roots are found in the Council of Trent (1545–1563). Through the work of the Jesuit priest, Francisco Ribera (1537–1591), the idea was put forth that the antichrist would appear in the last remnant of time of this earth's history.[242] This interpretation of

[237]"Key 73: No Violation," *Christianity Today*, March 16, 1973.

[238]Paul A. Pomerville, *The Third Force in Missions: A Pentecostal Contribution to Contemporary Mission Theology* (2016).

[239]A clear exposition of modern Spiritualism, the Charismatic Movement and the Three-fold Union is given in Norman Gulley's book *Christ is Coming!*, chapters 10, 11, and 42.

[240]Vinson Synan, *Charismatic Bridges*, pp. 8–14.

[241]*Selected Messages*, book 3, p. 410, emphasis added.

[242]LeRoy Froom, *Prophetic Faith of Our Fathers*, vol. 2, pp. 495–502; see also chapters 21–23 in particular. See also "Francisco Ribera," available at http://1ref.us/rr, accessed 2/27/2019.

antichrist was intended to repel the Protestants' claim that the papacy was the antichrist. Luther is reported to have said, "I know that the pope is Antichrist, and that his throne is that of Satan himself."[243]

Over the years, Ribera's theory evolved through John Nelson Darby, the Plymouth Brethren, and the Scofield Bible into present-day dispensationalism with its belief in the secret rapture. We hear much about the futurist view of the seventieth week of Daniel 9, which advocates the secret rapture, the tribulation, and the antichrist that is to appear during the seventieth week supposedly after the secret rapture. This has effectively removed the stigma of antichrist from the Roman Catholic Church, which the reformers unabashedly declared the church to be.[244] The way is now open for Protestants to accept Roman Catholicism both on common points of doctrine and on a common spiritual experience. "Papists, who boast of miracles as a certain sign of the true church, will be readily deceived by this wonder-working power; and Protestants, having cast away the shield of truth, will also be deluded."[245] One hundred years ago, we were told that the wonder-working power of spiritism would deceive Protestantism and that, together, they would clasp hands with Romanism.[246] Researchers who have observed this phenomenon characterize it as moving with "breathtaking speed" or "remarkable speed."[247] Ellen White wrote about what she foresaw: "The agencies of evil are combining their forces and consolidating. They are strengthening for the last great crisis. Great changes are soon to take place in our world, and the final movements will be rapid ones."[248] It is awe-inspiring to be living in the time of the fulfilling of prophecy. I would highly encourage everyone to look at the references given here.

---

[243] J. H. Merle D'Augbigne, D. D., *History of the Reformation of the Sixteenth Century*, Book 6, chap. 9.

[244] *The Great Controversy*, pp. 86, 87, 139–142.

[245] *The Great Controversy*, p. 588.

[246] *The Great Controversy*, p. 588.

[247] Mark A. Noll and Carolyn Nystrom, *Is The Reformation Over?*, pp. 69, 76.

[248] *Testimonies for the Church*, vol. 9, p. 11.

The third force

When I was pastoring in Newfoundland, Canada, in the 1970s, I came to know several Pentecostal ministers. Our church wanted to find a place of meeting for a company of Seventh-day Adventist believers in Stephenville. The only church that seemed to be available was the Pentecostal church. I had a friendly conversation with the pastor of the church about using their facility, and, as I left, he handed me a book, *They Speak with Other Tongues*. The author, John L. Sherrill, a writer for *Guideposts* magazine, enumerated the three streams of Christendom. He began, "By the time Dr. Van Dusen had finished digesting the information he had gathered on his trip, he was speaking of 'a third, mighty arm of Christendom,' standing boldly alongside the Catholic and Protestant arms. And at the hard, center core of this third force was the Pentecostal revival.... *Bishop Leslie Newbigin* in his book, *The Household of God*, listed three principal streams of life within the Christian Church. The first is Catholic. The second is Protestant. And the third is Pentecostal."[249]

Reading these words started me thinking. Seventh-day Adventists have long believed that, at the end of time, there would be a three-fold union in opposition to God.[250] Traditionally we have described these three entities in this three-fold union as "Catholicism," "apostate Protestantism," and "spiritism." Spiritualists claim to communicate with the dead. The phenomenon of spiritism, referred to in Isaiah 8:19, also included a manifestation of unintelligible "tongues." We read, "And when they say to you, 'Seek those who are mediums and wizards, who whisper and mutter,' should not a people seek their God? Should they seek the dead on behalf of the living?" Note that the medium spoke in unintelligible speech. Thus we see there is more to spiritism than merely communicating with the dead. Tongues manifestations were also involved.

---

[249] John L. Sherrill, *They Speak with Other Tongues* (1968), pp. 28, 65.
[250] Revelation 16:13, 14.

It is unwise to think Satan will use only one form of spiritism in the end time. Ellen White lists various forms of spiritism: mysterious rappings,[251] Christian Science,[252] the Emmanuel movement,[253] phrenology and animal magnetism,[254] modernized forms of ancient heathenism[255] presented in pleasing forms to imitate true Christianity,[256] oriental religions,[257] revival of demon worship,[258] theosophy,[259] the holy flesh movement in the Adventist church,[260] and pantheism.[261] Spiritism does not only deal with the dead but also with false concepts of God and the Holy Spirit.[262]

As I pursued this topic in my studies over the years, it dawned on me that the "fire from heaven" of Revelation 13:13 could be referring to the counterfeit of the true baptism of the Holy Spirit, which John the Baptist mentioned in Matthew 3:11. This modern-day "baptism in the spirit"[263] phenomenon seems to be what Ellen White was referring to as the "more pleasing forms of spiritism" that would profess faith in the Bible.[264] There is much that can be said about the more pleasing forms of spiritism.[265] The Apostle Paul wrote, "Now the Spirit expressly says that in latter times some will depart from the faith, giving heed to deceiving spirits and doctrines of demons" (1 Tim. 4:1).

---

[251] *Early Writings*, pp. 86–92.

[252] *Evangelism*, p. 606.

[253] *Evangelism*, p. 606; see also "The Emmanuel Movement," *The Review and Herald*, vol. 86, nos. 9, 10, 11 (Washington, D.C., 1909); Ellen G. White Research Center, file DF 2170, Andrews University, Berrien Springs, Michigan.

[254] *Selected Messages*, vol. 2, p. 352.

[255] *The Desire of Ages*, p. 258.

[256] *Evangelism*, p. 606; *The Great Controversy*, p. 588.

[257] *Evangelism*, p. 606.

[258] *Patriarchs and Prophets*, p. 686.

[259] *Prophets and Kings*, p. 210.

[260] *Evangelism*, p. 594; *Selected Messages*, vol. 2, pp. 31, 36.

[261] *Testimonies for the Church*, vol. 8, p. 291.

[262] *Evangelism*, p. 601.

[263] Also referred to as the "baptism of fire." See Michael Harper, *The Baptism of Fire* (1970).

[264] *Evangelism*, p. 606; see also *The Great Controversy*, p. 588.

[265] Allan Freed, *What's All the Confusion about Tongues?* File DF311, Research Center, James White Library, Andrews University, Berrien Springs, MI.

Consider the following thought from the pen of Ellen White: "A belief in spiritual manifestations opens the door to seducing spirits and doctrines of devils, and thus the influence of evil angels will be felt in the churches."[266] Notice that she said "churches" and not just "church." In 1956, Pentecostalism made its way into the Protestant churches as the charismatic movement.[267] Then, in 1967, the charismatic phenomenon crossed over into the Catholic Church at Duquesne University and at Notre Dame University in South Bend, Indiana.[268] Killian McDonnell stated, "Within Catholicism Pentecostalism has met with considerably less resistance than it has within the historic Protestant churches, partly because the concept of the 'wondrous' is more at home in Catholicism than in mainstream Protestantism."[269] Kevin and Dorothy Ranaghan said of David Wilkerson's account of the baptism of the Spirit: "It was very old doctrine, it was very traditional doctrine, it was very Catholic doctrine."[270]

Again, I was impressed by what I read in *The Great Controversy*, page 588, "And as the spirits will profess faith in the Bible, and manifest respect for the institutions of the church, their work will be accepted as a manifestation of divine power.... Papists, who boast of miracles as a certain sign of the true church will be readily deceived by this wonder-working power." In 1980, the Word of Faith movement emerged within the charismatic movement.[271] Its preachers "frequently claim revelation knowledge that brings 'correctives' to Paul's negative confessions. They claim that Paul did not have the true faith message."[272] It is enlightening also that Ellen White wrote that, "to take the place of the word of God," Satan "holds

---

[266] *The Great Controversy*, p. 603.

[267] McCandlish Phillips, "And there appeared to them tongues of fire," *Saturday Evening Post*, May 16, 1964.

[268] Kilian McDonnell, O.S.B., *Catholic Pentecostalism: Problems in Evaluation* (1971), p. 3; Kevin and Dorothy Ranaghan, *Catholic Pentecostals* (1969).

[269] Kilian McDonnell, O.S.B., *Catholic Pentecostalism: Problems in Evaluation* (1971), p. 31.

[270] Kevin and Dorothy Ranaghan, *Catholic Pentecostals* (1969), pp. 9, 10.

[271] Robert M. Bowman, Jr., "Word-Faith Movement," available at http://1ref.us/rs, accessed 2/27/2019.

[272] Charles Farah, "American Pentecostals: What They Believe," *Christianity Today*, Oct. 16, 1987, p. 23; James R. Goff, Jr., "The Faith that Claims," *Christianity Today*, Feb. 19, 1990, p. 20.

out spiritual manifestations. Here is a channel wholly under his control; by this means he can make the world believe what he will."[273]

The story of Elijah on Mount Carmel and the prophecy of John the Baptist speak of "fire" as a demonstration of the power of God. However, in the end-time there will be a false fire from heaven (Rev. 13:13, 14).[274] It is amazing how often the baptism of the Spirit is referred to in charismatic circles as the "baptism of fire." That phrase has found its way into literature and titles of books. This false fire will unite Christendom in a three-fold union. "And I saw three unclean spirits like frogs coming out of the mouth of the dragon, out of the mouth of the beast, and out of the mouth of the false prophet. For they are spirits of demons, performing signs, which go out to the kings of the earth and of the whole world, to gather them to the battle of that great day of God Almighty" (Rev. 16:13, 14). The editors of *These Times* magazine saw these verses as a "flashback, showing how Babylon [that is, the three-fold union of the dragon, the beast, and the false prophet] secured her power prior to the sixth plague" and that there would be a "great spiritualistic revival" uniting Christendom on such points of doctrine as they hold in common.[275] These words are now fulfilling before our very eyes.[276]

A clear indication of the judgment of the living

As this three-fold union is forming, judgment will be going on, for judgment is implied in Revelation 16:15, where it is parenthetically mentioned with the formation of the three-fold union. It reads, "Behold, I am coming as a thief, blessed is he who watches and keeps his garments"

---

[273] *Darkness before Dawn*, p. 21.

[274] *The Great Controversy*, p. 612.

[275] "The Amazing Prophecies of Daniel and Revelation," *These Times*, Special Issue (1983), p. 51; see also *The Great Controversy*, p. 445.

[276] Dateline: "Lutherans, Catholics, Methodists, Reformed, and Anglicans 'drawn into deeper communion'," *Ministry*, December 2017, p. 4.

(Rev. 16:15). Ellen White clearly understood the passing of the judgment in heaven from the dead to the living as happening like a thief in the night. "The judgment is now passing in the sanctuary above.... Soon—none know how soon—it will pass to the cases of the living.... At this time above all others it behooves every soul to heed the Saviour's admonition: ... 'If therefore thou shalt not watch, I will come on thee as a thief, and thou shalt not know what hour I will come upon thee.' Revelation 3:3."[277] The three-fold union will have been formed just before the close of probation, and inserted in the formation of this union is the thief-in-the-night experience—the final atonement for the living commonly called the judgment of the living.[278]

Another indication

And yet, there is another phenomenon that will be evident just before the close of probation that will indicate the nearness of the end. I will start with an overture made by the charismatic movement. In 1971, someone sent me the *Voice* magazine from the Full Gospel Businessmen's Fellowship International. It was given to me and other Adventist pastors with the express purpose of taking the charismatic movement into the Seventh-day Adventist Church.[279] Now that I am on this side of things, I can see how it has been working. Music has played a big part in their mission. That which appeals to the emotions has been the main focus. Praise music and the lifting of hands in worship originated in modern churches today through the influence of the charismatic movement with justification from the book of Psalms.

This music started with the Jesus Movement (the youth part of the charismatic movement) to which rock and roll artists, notably Larry

---

[277] *The Great Controversy*, pp. 490, 491.

[278] *The Great Controversy*, pp. 490, 491; Rev. 16:13–16; *The Great Controversy*, p. 588.

[279] See also Roland R. Hegstad, *As the Spirit Speaks* (1973), p. 13ff.

Norman, were converted.[280] Larry Norman is known as the father of gospel rock. He popularized the sentiment, "Why should the Devil have all the good music?" Gospel rock moves easily with secular music on the pop charts as well as in the churches.[281] With many contemporary worship songs, there is little difference between sacred and secular musical sounds. Many of the lyrics can either praise and extol God or they can describe contemporary life. The songs that traverse the pop charts can easily apply to self, to a boyfriend or a girlfriend, to the Holy Spirit, or to God. The double meaning of much of it can suit almost anyone's taste. Consequently, praise services like these have entered virtually every denomination's worship format with rhythms and instruments of the pop music genre.[282] We must be discerning and know that religious "excitement is not favorable to growth in grace, to true purity and sanctification of the spirit."[283]

It is not for me to judge what constitutes acceptable worship music. One thing I know, however, is that, if it confuses me so that I cannot discern whether it is presenting clear biblical truth, then I am treading on dangerous ground.[284] If the

> **"***If the music we listen to affects us in such a way that we "cannot tell what" we "formerly knew regarding Bible principles," then we may know it is not of God.***"**

music we listen to affects us in such a way that we "cannot tell what" we "formerly knew regarding Bible principles," then we may know it is not of God.[285] This is a serious matter, and we must be honest with ourselves. The

---

[280] Larry David Norman (1947–2008) was an American musician, singer, songwriter, record label owner, and record producer. He is considered to be one of the pioneers of Christian rock music, releasing more than 100 albums. (Wikipedia, Dec. 2017). For a more recent exposé of the media world see "Media on the Brain - Mini Seminar," available at http://1ref.us/rt, accessed 2/27/2019.

[281] That is, the musical group "Skillet," etc.

[282] "Contemporary Christian music," available at http://1ref.us/ru, accessed 2/27/2019.

[283] *Selected Messages*, vol. 2, p. 35.

[284] *Last Day Events*, p. 159.

[285] *Selected Messages*, vol. 2, p. 37.

Apostle John wrote, "Do not love the world or the things in the world. If anyone loves the world, the love of the Father is not in him" (1 John 2:15). So what is the answer? "With divine help we are to form our opinions for ourselves as we are to answer for ourselves before God."[286]

Right now you may be saying, "So what!" Though the issue of music may not seem important to you, I am calling attention to it because of the comments Ellen White made concerning the music at an Indiana camp meeting, sometime around 1900. She identified the loud music as a "bedlam of noise" that "shocks the senses and perverts that which if conducted aright might be a blessing." Then she went on to make a prediction, "The powers of satanic agencies blend with the din and noise, to have a carnival, and this is termed the Holy Spirit's working.... Those things which have been in the past will be in the future. Satan will make music a snare by the way in which it is conducted."[287] As a guide to what would be appropriate, the following counsel is given: "God's work is ever characterized by calmness and dignity."[288]

Ellen White saw, however (and this is the main point), that this type of music would be popular in the churches just before the close of probation.[289] What takes place just before the close of probation? It is the judgment of the living. The judgment of those who died professing faith in Christ started in 1844, and, in the natural course of things, it will end when the judgment moves on to those who are alive and profess faith in the name of our Savior. All these things I have mentioned here tell me we are now in the judgment of the living—the process of the final at-onement with Jesus. This is but the beginning of what will culminate in legislation intended to force people everywhere to worship the beast and his image as portrayed in Revelation 13.[290]

---

[286] *The Great Controversy*, p. 598.

[287] *Selected Messages*, vol. 2, pp. 36, 38.

[288] *Selected Messages*, vol. 2, p. 42.

[289] *Selected Messages*, vol. 2, pp. 35–38; see also Paul Hamel, *Ellen White and Music* (1976), pp. 42–48.

[290] Revelation 13:12, 15; see also Revelation 14:9, 11.

More on the three-fold union

Now let us turn to something more recent—Pope Francis calling charismatics to unite with Rome.[291] Tony Palmer of the Episcopal/Anglican church became the emissary of the Vatican to facilitate this union.[292] Since nearly all Protestants in America and elsewhere have espoused the seventieth week theory of biblical interpretation, the papacy is no longer viewed as the antichrist as the reformers so viewed it.[293]

Even in the 1970s at the Ministerial Association in the city where I pastored, an Evangelical Lutheran pastor said, "I am a Protestant, but I am not protesting." Consequently, it came as no surprise that in 1999 the Lutherans and the Catholics signed a document that Tony Palmer said ended the Protestant Reformation.[294] In speaking to a conference of 1,500 charismatic pastors, Palmer said, "Brothers and Sisters, Luther's protest is over—is yours?"[295] Then he added, "If there is no more protest, how can there be a protestant church? ... The protest is over." Then he invoked John chapter 17 to support the view that the churches are fulfilling the prayer of Christ for unity. In the charismatic renewal, the emphasis is not only on the gifts of the Spirit but overwhelmingly on the "presence of Jesus." Palmer said that the glory of God is the unifying principle: "It is the glory that glues us together, not the doctrines.... God will sort out all our doctrines when we get upstairs"—that is, when we get to heaven.[296]

---

[291] Pope Francis, "Pope Francis Sends Video Message to Kenneth Copeland – Lets Unite," available at http://1ref.us/km, accessed 2/27/2019.

[292] The angels most obviously are holding the four winds of strife (Rev. 7:1–3). Tony Palmer died as a result of a motorcycle accident July 20, 2014.

[293] *The Great Controversy*, pp. 139, 141. The 70th week theory places a gap of hundreds of years between sixty-ninth and seventieth week of Daniel 9, and identifies the "anointed one" as a false messiah.

[294] For a discussion of this document, see Clifford Goldstein, *The Great Compromise* (2001), chaps. 1 and 2. This book is also an excellent explanation of justification by faith.

[295] Tony Palmer, "Pope Francis Sends Video Message to Kenneth Copeland – Lets Unite," available at http://1ref.us/km, accessed 2/27/2019.

[296] Tony Palmer, "Pope Francis Sends Video Message to Kenneth Copeland – Lets Unite," available at http://1ref.us/km, accessed 2/27/2019.

Bishop Tony Palmer referenced the Elijah message (Mal. 4:5-6), concerning the turning of the hearts of the fathers to the children and of the children to the fathers, to describe what he believed to be fulfilling as the Protestant churches come back to Rome and the Roman church welcomes them back. Pope Francis said, "Tears will unite us." God "will complete this miracle of unity." Palmer rejoiced in the fact that Pope Francis is charismatic. At the end of this session of the conference, Kenneth Copeland praised both the pope and Tony Palmer for their work in the Lord. Then, in response to the pope's request for prayer, Copeland prayed for him. Copeland was ecstatic and said that we cannot simply pray in human language. So, the whole conference of 1,500 attendees broke out into prayer in "tongues." At the end of the prayer, Copeland said to the pope, "Thank you, Sir. We do bless you! We receive your blessing. It's very, very important to us."[297]

> **"Clearly an extraordinary three-fold union is forming in a way that we did not anticipate."**

Clearly an extraordinary three-fold union is forming in a way that we did not anticipate.

As we have noted, embedded in this three-fold union is the process of the thief-in-the-night experience—the judgment of the living, or, as it may be called, the *final at-onement* of Jesus with His people.[298] Involved in this judgment is the putting away of sin from our lives and the blotting out of the record of sin in the heavenly sanctuary for God's people.[299] Our part is to "cleanse ourselves from all filthiness of the flesh and spirit, perfecting holiness in the fear of God" (2 Cor. 7:1). We do this by claiming the promise of 1 John 1:9, and, by repentance and faith, sending all our sins on "beforehand to judgment" where they "may be blotted out, so that times of refreshing may come from the presence of the Lord."[300]

---

[297] Kenneth Copeland, "Pope Francis Sends Video Message to Kenneth Copeland – Lets Unite," available at http://1ref.us/km, accessed 2/27/2019.

[298] Revelation 16:13–15; 3:3; Matthew 24:37–43; *Testimonies for Ministers*, pp. 234, 235; *The Great Controversy*, pp. 490, 491.

[299] *The Great Controversy*, p. 620.

[300] 1 Timothy 5:24, KJV; Acts 3:19; *The Great Controversy*, pp. 483–485.

Chapter 13

An Evaluation of the True and False Latter Rain

The thief-in-the-night experience, the coming of the Comforter as the latter rain, the judgment of the living, and the blotting out of sin are all very much related. Jesus said, "The words that I speak to you are spirit, and they are life" (John 6:63). Proverbs 1:23 says, "I will pour out my spirit on you; I will make my words known to you." On the day of Pentecost, all those who were gathered to listen to the preaching of the apostles heard the words of salvation spoken in their own languages (Acts 2:11). Later, in answer to their prayer, the Holy Spirit came upon them "and they spoke the word of God with boldness" (Acts 4:31). The Holy Spirit is always allied with not only living the Christian life but with the proclamation of the word of God. The latter rain is not an emotional high; it is spreading the good news of God's Word throughout the world with such clarity that all who are willing will come to a knowledge of God's truth for this time.[301] "For the earth shall be full of the knowledge of the LORD as the waters cover the sea" (Isa. 11:9).

Another assessment of spiritism

"But," someone may ask, "what about the 'unknown tongue' in 1 Corinthians 12–14?" To answer this question, we must first recognize that the word

---

[301] Letter 11b, 1892, July 17, 1892, to S. N. Haskell.

"unknown" is not in the original—it is added. In the King James Version, added words are italicized. Second, in this epistle, Paul is seeking to bring a manifestation of a false experience of tongues under the control of the true gift of tongues. Notice he begins this passage referencing "dumb idols." He wrote: "Now concerning spiritual gifts, brethren, I do not want you to be ignorant: You know that you were Gentiles, carried away to these dumb idols, however you were led" (1 Cor. 12:1, 2). "Dumb idols" are idols that cannot speak. He is clearly referring to their experience in idol worship before they became Christians. They were carried along in the frenzy of idol worship—worship which included unknown gibberish.[302] Paul, in harmony with his usual procedure, defines the true gifts first, in chapter 12, before dealing with the problem of the false gift in chapter 14.

"Tongues," or "language," in this passage is *glōssa*. The phrase in the Greek of 1 Corinthians 12:10 and 28 is *genē glōssōn*. *Glōssōn* means "tongues" or languages, the same as in Revelation 14:6, where *glōssan* is translated "tongue." *Genē* describes *glōssōn* and is translated "kind." However, the root form of *genē* is *genos*, which means "offspring," "family," "race," "nation," "class," or "kind." Used as it is in this passage, it would mean "familial," "racial," "national," or "kindred." The *glōssōn* that Paul is describing is national languages, which is the true gift of "tongues." Thus, the true gift of tongues is real languages and the translation of those real languages (1 Cor. 12:10; Acts 2:4, 11). Scripture and Ellen White strongly agree that the "unknown tongue" is unknown, for it is not only unknown to man but also to God.[303]

Again you may ask, "When a person speaks in an unknown tongue, didn't Paul say he is speaking to God?" In the original language of 1 Corinthians 12–14, wherever the true God is mentioned, it is with the definite article—which would literally be translated "the God" or some other designation that points to specificity. 1 Corinthians 14:2 is the only instance in this whole passage, from chapter 12 to 14, that uses the word "god" without

---

[302] Gerhard Kittel, ed., *Theological Dictionary of the New Testament*, vol. 1, translated and edited by Geoffrey W. Bromiley (1964), p. 723.
[303] 1 Corinthians 14:9; *Testimonies for the Church*, vol. 1, p. 412.

the definite article. Used in this way, it generally means either a deity or "a god" in a more generic sense. This is how pagans would refer to deity.[304]

I have concluded, after a close study of this passage of Scripture, that both a true and a false phenomenon of tongues was manifest at Corinth.[305] The reasons I have come to this conclusion are: (1) Paul testifies to the true gift of tongues in 1 Corinthians 1:5 and 6, "That you were enriched in everything by Him in all utterance [speech] and all knowledge, even as the testimony of Christ [the spirit of prophecy, Rev. 19:10] was confirmed in you." (2) Some of the believers in Corinth had written to Paul for clarification on several controversies—for example, sexual immorality (1 Cor. 5:1), marriage (1 Cor. 7:1), foods offered to idols (1 Cor. 8:1), the communion service (1 Cor. 11:17, 18), and tongues (1 Cor. 12:1–14). "In Corinth ... glossolalia is an unintelligible ecstatic utterance. ... Parallels may be found for this phenomenon in various forms and at various periods and places in religious history."[306]

We have been told, "It is often the case that the most precious truth appears to lie close by the side of fatal errors."[307] It should be remembered that wherever God is working Satan

> **"Satan employed the spiritual phenomenon of tongues for centuries before the time of the church in Corinth."**

tries to bring in a counterfeit to distract from the blessing and appreciation of truth. Satan employed the spiritual phenomenon of tongues for centuries before the time of the church in Corinth, and he has employed it at later times even within Islam.[308] Undeniably, a gibberish form of spiritism is evidenced in Isaiah 8:19.

---

[304] For explanation of 1 Corinthian 14:2, see H. E. Dana, Th.D., Julian R. Mantey, Th.D., D.D., *A Manual Grammar of the Greek New Testament* (1962), pp. 139, 140.

[305] Fernando Chaij, *The Impending Drama*, chapter 84; concerning false tongues, which was a carry-over from pagan religions, see Gerhard Kittel, ed., *Theological Dictionary of the New Testament*, vol. 1, p. 722.

[306] Gerhard Kittel, ed., *Theological Dictionary of the New Testament*, vol. 1, p. 722.

[307] Ms. 100, 1893; *The Great Controversy*, pp. 186, 464, 528.

[308] Norman Gulley, *Christ is Coming!* (1998), p. 143.

Following the right Spirit is a crucial part of the judgment of the living—our final at-onement with Christ. It is also very much a part of the experience of the latter rain. The judgment of the living, the blotting out of sin, and the refreshing, which is the perfecting latter rain of the Holy Spirit, are all interrelated.[309] The Apostle Peter says, "The appointed time of the judgment [is] to start from the household of God; now since first from us, what [will be] the end of those who are disobeying the gospel of God" (1 Peter 4:17, author's translation). This text tells me the judgment has a starting point from which it proceeds. It begins with God's people. (See also the representation of judgment in Ezekiel 9.) The judgment, or final atonement, is the process of our merciful God bringing His people fully into harmony with the great principles of His holy law, which is the foundation of His character and government. The starting point is with those who have professed to believe in God's saving grace. From this group it proceeds through every generation and ends with the final eradication of sin and sinners.

During the times of ancient Israel, sins were blotted out as they were removed from the sanctuary *and* the people on the Day of Atonement (Lev. 16). It was a time of judgment because all who would not cooperate by confession and repentance in sending their sins beforehand to the sanctuary received judgment to be "cut off" (Lev. 23:24–29).[310] There are a number of things about the antitypical Day of Atonement in which we are now living that require our attention. First, it is apparent from both Scripture and the Spirit of Prophecy that sins will be blotted out of the records in the heavenly sanctuary with a corresponding removal from the conscience of the believer. Paul says, "How much more shall the blood of Christ, who through the eternal Spirit offered Himself without spot to God, cleanse your conscience from dead works to serve the living God?" (Heb. 9:14; see also 10:1, 2). Ellen White picks up on this sanctuary imagery, applying it to the time of trouble after probation has closed. Describing those whose

---

309 *The Great Controversy*, pp. 483, 485.
310 Pröbstle, p. 62, especially note 1; see also 1 Timothy 5:24, KJV.

sins have been blotted out in the judgment, she says: "But while they have a deep sense of their unworthiness, they have no concealed wrongs to reveal. Their sins have gone beforehand to judgment and have been blotted out, and they cannot bring them to remembrance."[311] In the judgment, there is a connection between the latter rain, the blotting out of sin, the cleansing of the heavenly sanctuary, and the cleansing of the conscience. The Apostle Peter says, "Repent and be converted that your sins may be blotted out when the times of refreshing shall come from the presence of the Lord." The "times of refreshing" are also known as the time when the "latter rain" will be poured out upon those who have prepared for it (Acts 3:19, KJV).[312]

Furthermore, Ellen White wrote, "It is impossible that the sins of men should be blotted out until after the judgment at which their cases are to be investigated."[313] This is the same as it was in the typical service. On the Day of Atonement, the Israelites were to send their sins on to judgment by confession and repentance. Then, their sins were blotted out through the blood of the Lord's goat and placed on the head of the scapegoat. The scapegoat was then taken into the wilderness nevermore to come into the camp of Israel (Lev. 16). It is easy to see the close connection of these three events—the judgment of the living as the Day of Atonement for the living, the refreshing of the latter rain, and the blotting out of sin.

What stimulated my interest in this subject was Ellen White's statement that, if we are waiting for the latter rain to change us or for Sunday legislation to wake us up, we are making a terrible mistake. "Many have in a great measure failed to receive the former rain. They have not obtained all the benefits that God has thus provided for them. They expect that the latter rain will supply the lack. When the richest abundance of grace shall be bestowed, they intend to open their hearts to receive it. *They are making a terrible mistake.*"[314] The mistake of which she speaks would be in not

---

[311] *The Great Controversy*, p. 620.
[312] *Early Writings*, p. 71; *The Great Controversy*, p. 611.
[313] *The Great Controversy*, p. 485.
[314] *Testimonies for Ministers*, p. 507, emphasis added.

having been diligent in sending our sins "on beforehand to judgment" by confession and repentance so that they *may* be blotted out when the latter rain comes. It could be falling all around, but we would not recognize it because we have not cooperated with Christ and followed Him by faith in His mediatorial work for us in the heavenly sanctuary.[315] Certainly this is a call for us to heed Paul's admonition, "Examine yourselves as to whether you are in the faith" (2 Cor. 13:5). How sad it will be for those who have neglected the needful preparation for receiving the final outpouring of the Holy Spirit!

The purpose of the latter rain

The next question to come to mind is: What *is* the purpose of the latter rain, and how do I prepare for it? In Scripture, the metaphor of rain symbolizes the showers of the Holy Spirit upon the church. Since the latter rain ripens the crop, it is logical it can only ripen grain that has already been produced. The early rain germinates the seed and produces a perfect plant at every stage of its growth.[316] Certainly we do not expect the tiny plant that has just sprouted through the crust of the earth to be mature. Yet, it is a perfect tiny sprout. This is an apt metaphor for Christian perfection. Our growth in Christ can be perfect at every stage. Indeed, Ellen White stated that we can be perfect because our sins are perfectly forgiven.[317] And, again, Christ wants us to be as perfectly for Him in this world as He is perfectly for us in the heavenly sanctuary.[318] That is, He wants us to be perfectly for Christ at every stage of existence in our Christian walk of life. This kind of perfection can mark every stage—"first the blade, then the head, after that the full grain in the head" (Mark 4:28). This is what the latter rain brings to fruition.

---

[315] *Testimonies for Ministers*, p. 507; *The Great Controversy*, p. 430.
[316] *Christ's Object Lessons*, p. 82.
[317] *Selected Messages*, vol. 2, p. 32.
[318] *Acts of the Apostles*, p. 566.

So then, it is the latter rain that ripens the grain which has already been produced in the Christian's character under the early rain of the Holy Spirit. Our daily walk with Christ is sanctification, which also may be described as Christian character development. We often think of character as outward conduct and expect that behavior modification will produce a noble character. But, character comes from within. It is a *quality of the soul* revealed in the conduct.[319] Ellen White insightfully stated, "Thoughts and feelings combined make up the moral character."[320] We may modify our outward behavior, but that is not character development. The Pharisees did as much. God wants us to abide in Christ and let His love dwell in our hearts. Then "our feelings, our thoughts, our actions, will be in harmony with the will of God. The sanctified heart is in harmony with the precepts of God's law."[321] "As we seek God for the Holy Spirit," through Christ's righteousness mediated for us in the heavenly sanctuary, "it will work in us meekness, humbleness of mind, a conscious dependence upon God for the perfecting latter rain."[322] Notice that the early rain has already done its work, and it is the latter rain that perfects our growth in Christ.

> **"*I must never forget that sin is blotted out in the antitypical sanctuary service—not when Christ returns.*"**

In a spiritual sense, the latter rain can only blot out the sins of which I have repented and of which the record has been covered by the blood and righteousness of Christ. If I cherish sin in my life and refuse to give up what the Holy Spirit convicts me of and do not let Jesus cleanse me from all unrighteousness (1 John 1:7–9), I will perish with my sin. Sin cannot be taken to heaven (Gal. 5:21; 1 Cor. 6:9, 10; 15:50). It must be dealt with

---

[319] *Child Guidance*, p. 161.
[320] *In Heavenly Places*, p. 164.
[321] *Acts of the Apostles*, p. 563.
[322] *The Faith I Live By*, p. 334.

here in this life. I must never forget that sin is blotted out in the antitypical sanctuary service—not when Christ returns (Heb. 9:28).[323]

The Christian culture of today is all about the cross, and it is true the cross is the center around which all other truths cluster—including Christ's high priestly ministry for us in the heavenly sanctuary (Rom. 8:34).[324] Nonetheless, if we turn away from the work our Wonderful Judge and High Priest is doing for us in the heavenly sanctuary and fail to cooperate with Him by repentance and faith in sending all our sins on beforehand to judgment to be covered with His blood, and if we fail to let Him cleanse us from all unrighteousness, we have, in effect, trampled the sacrifice of the cross, the blood of the Son of God, underfoot (Heb. 6:6; 10:29). We must accept the full gospel of our Lord and Savior Jesus Christ, and that includes His High Priestly ministry for us in the heavenly sanctuary.

When the latter rain comes, it also gives power for witnessing, and it gives boldness in proclaiming the truth as it is in Jesus (Acts 4:31). Such boldness is without fear of consequences. With a "loud voice," those who have received the latter rain will proclaim that Babylon is fallen and is full of every evil spirit (Rev. 18:1–5). They will reveal fully the deceptions of the three-fold union and the work of the false latter rain. As stated above, with reference to Proverbs 1:23, the work of the latter rain will be to make God's Word so plain that everyone who hears it will be brought to a decision for or against the truth of His holy law, as manifest in Christ our righteousness.[325] This truth will be proclaimed throughout the entire world. Those who decide for God's truth will be sealed with the seal of the living God.[326]

As we have grown in the "grace and the knowledge of our Lord and Savior," we become settled into the "truth as it is in Jesus." Growing to reflect the image of Jesus in what we think, love, and do, we will attain

---

[323] See also the *Amplified Bible, Common English Bible,* and NET versions.

[324] *Evangelism,* p. 190.

[325] *Testimonies for the Church,* vol. 6, p. 19.

[326] *The Great Controversy,* p. 605.

emotional maturity in accordance with 1 Corinthians 13 and our life will be found to be in harmony with His holy law (James 2:12; 1:25; Rom. 13:8–10). It is the Holy Spirit that writes and seals the law of God in our hearts (2 Cor. 3:3; Isa. 8:16).[327] With the holy law of God sealed in our hearts, the end result is that our sins are blotted out—never again to be remembered (Isa. 43:25). The New Covenant experience of having the holy law of God written in our hearts is a progressive work, having its full result in the final judgment when God's promise of the New Covenant has been fulfilled, "I will be merciful to their unrighteousness, and their sins and their lawless deeds I will remember no more" (Heb. 8:12).

The interesting part of all this is we are unaware the judgment is taking place. Our focus has been not on ourselves but on Christ and His righteousness on our behalf in the heavenly sanctuary. The closer we come to Jesus the more sinful we see ourselves to be.[328] After probation closes, we cannot bring any specific sin to remembrance, even though we have such an awful awareness of the sinfulness of sin. During the seven last plagues, "if the people of God had unconfessed sins to appear before them … they could not have confidence to plead with God for deliverance. But while they have a deep sense of their unworthiness, they have no concealed wrongs to reveal. Their sins have gone beforehand to judgment and have been blotted out, and they cannot bring them to remembrance."[329] Their consciences have been purged from the remembrance of sin through the blood of Christ during the final atonement in the heavenly sanctuary (Heb. 9:9–14; 10:1, 2). For them, the latter rain has been the "perfecting latter rain."[330] It has prepared the church to stand during the trying hour of the seven last plagues that are to fall upon the earth and to live in the sight of a holy God without a mediator.[331]

---

[327] *The Great Controversy*, p. 452.

[328] *Steps to Christ*, p. 64.

[329] *The Great Controversy*, p. 620; it would be well to meditate on the whole chapter and know for oneself what it means that "sins go beforehand to judgment."

[330] *Review and Herald*, March 2, 1897.

[331] *The Great Controversy*, pp. 613, 614.

The purpose of this trying hour for God's people is to bring the at-onement to completion. The image of Jesus is perfectly reflected in us that He may come and take us home to be with Him in heaven. Even though we have reflected the image of Jesus as we have grown in the graces of the Christian life—first the blade than the ear, and then the full corn in the ear—yet, it is only under the sixth plague, after probation has closed, that we reflect the image of Jesus fully. We pass through the trying hour of the seven last plagues because our "earthliness" needs to be "consumed, that the image of Christ may be perfectly reflected."[332] Then, when Christ sees His moral image—His character—perfectly reproduced in us, He will come to take us home to heaven.[333] Christ's imputed righteousness, into which we are sealed, has become our imparted righteousness.

There is much more that could be said about the outpouring of the Holy Spirit in the latter rain. Our denomination, in the past few years, has made a concerted effort to have the membership pray for the outpouring of the Holy Spirit in latter rain power. The little book *True Revival: The Church's Greatest Need* is one of the best books I have ever read for calling us to revival and readiness for the latter rain—especially the first chapter.[334] Is it not time we honor the call in this little book and take its message into our very lives so that each one of us may be ready for the closing events of this earth's history?

I have given in this section the essential points regarding the judgment of the living—the final at-onement of the living with Christ our redeemer. Indeed, this is the final reconciliation of redeemed sinners to a holy God. Yet, one thing remains. "For our citizenship is in heaven, from which we also eagerly wait for the Savior, the Lord Jesus Christ, who will transform our lowly body that it may be conformed to His glorious body, according to the working by which He is able even to subdue all things to Himself" (Phil. 3:20, 21).

---

[332] *The Great Controversy*, p. 621.
[333] *Christ's Object Lessons*, p. 69.
[334] Ellen G. White, *True Revival: The Church's Greatest Need* (2010).

O, to grace how great a debtor,
Daily I'm constrained to be!
Let thy goodness, like a fetter,
Bind me closer still to thee.
Prone to wander, Lord, I feel it,
Prone to leave the God I love;
Here's my heart—O, take and seal it;
Seal it for thy courts above.[335]

---

[335] Robert Robinson, "Come Thou Fount of Every Blessing," *Seventh-day Adventist Hymnal* (1985), hymn no. 334.

CHRIST OUR RIGHTEOUSNESS ALL THROUGH ETERNITY

Chapter 14

Ready for Heaven

Many signs of Christ's return are fulfilling all around us. As I have shown in the preceding chapters, there are some signs we don't often think about. That the three-fold union has been formed is indication that we are in the final at-onement of the living. The shift in style in religious music is a fulfillment of what Ellen White saw would happen just before the close of probation. Now the words of Jesus are rapidly fulfilling also, "And this gospel of the kingdom will be preached in all the world as a witness to all the nations, and then the end will come" (Matt. 24:14). Never has the world been blanketed with the good news of salvation as it is now. The Adventist church has many mediums for proclaiming Christ to the world. Hope Channel and its subsidiaries, 3ABN channels, Amazing Facts, Loma Linda University channels, Adventist World Radio, among others are going over the airwaves like the three angels flying in the midst of heaven. Also, besides the regular mission activity of the church, such programs as Adventist Frontier Missions and Advocates for Southeast Asians and the Persecuted are reaching remote people groups. Internet programs on YouTube, podcasts, iPhones, and other forms of social media have unfathomable latitude. Today the call is being given, "All things are ready. Come to the wedding" (Matt. 22:4). For God will "finish the work and cut it short in righteousness" (Rom. 9:28).

Before Christ's return

God is in charge of our salvation. All that He asks of us is that we cooperate with Him. Adam and Eve failed to cooperate, and they fell from grace.

Over and over again the Israelites failed to cooperate with Him—both during and after God led them out of Egypt. As a result, a whole generation perished in their wilderness journey. We see, throughout Scripture, examples of those who have and those who have not cooperated with our Savior. In every case, the struggle has been with selfish human nature. Indeed, the greatest battle we have to wage is the battle with self. Our natural inclination is to non-cooperation. We continually seek to justify ourselves, much like the lawyer in Luke 10:29. But Jesus says, "Without Me you can do nothing" (John 15:5). Our only hope of salvation is in Christ our righteousness interceding for us in the heavenly sanctuary and the Holy Spirit working in and through us.[336] When we look to Jesus, the Holy Spirit will lead us home.

There is no lack on God's part. Jesus said, "All authority has been given to Me in heaven and on earth" (Matt. 28:18). The Holy Spirit is Christ's representative on earth, and He is given to us so that we may overcome every hereditary and cultivated tendency to evil.[337] Jesus gave His life for the church "that He might sanctify and cleanse her with the washing of water by the word, that He might present her to Himself a glorious church, not having spot or wrinkle or any such thing, but that she should be holy and without blemish" (Eph. 5:26, 27).

So how do we cooperate with God to be ready for Christ's return? One thing is clear—God wants us to "pursue peace with all people, and holiness, without which no one will see the Lord" (Heb. 12:14). Moreover, Paul's prayer was that our "whole spirit, soul, and body be preserved blameless at the coming of our Lord Jesus Christ" (1 Thess. 5:23).

In this little volume I have tried to set forth God's purpose and plan for our redemption from the ruin that sin has made. Jesus prayed that we be with Him in glory. "Father, I desire that they also whom You gave Me may be with Me where I am, that they may behold My glory which You have given Me" (John 17:24). God gave us Jesus. Jesus gave His life, and

---

[336] *Steps to Christ*, p. 63.
[337] *The Desire of Ages*, pp. 669, 671.

He gives the Holy Spirit to all who accept God's plan for their salvation. The holy angels are given as "ministering spirits sent forth to minister for those who will inherit salvation" (Heb. 1:14). All heaven is involved in the restoration of all things. It is God's call to us to cooperate with all heaven that we might be with Him in glory. He created us. He redeemed us. He wants us to know Him as our personal, loving heavenly Father—first in heaven and then in the earth made new.

So again, how *do* we cooperate with our blessed Lord so we can be ready for His return? First, we come to Jesus just as we are through the study of God's Word (2 Tim. 2:15), for in it is revealed God's plan for us. Then, we respond to the Holy Spirit through the Word, and the Spirit leads us to Christ who is ministering His righteousness for us in the heavenly sanctuary. The Holy Spirit convicts us of sin and points us to Jesus as our Savior. We confess our sins, and the Holy Spirit cleanses us from all sin. Through "repentance toward God and faith toward our Lord Jesus Christ" (Acts 20:21) we send all our sins on beforehand to judgment so that Jesus Himself can blot them out of the records of heaven and out of any

> *"Sin is to be dealt with in this life; it cannot be carried over into heaven."*

remembrance for His own name's sake, sealing us for eternity with the seal of the living God, which is the perfecting latter rain of the Spirit. Sin is to be dealt with in this life; it cannot be carried over into heaven (1 Cor. 6:9, 10; Gal. 5:21). We are to let the Holy Spirit sanctify our thoughts and feelings, which make up the moral character we take from this life to the next.[338]

The purpose of salvation is to restore in us the character of Adam before his fall. Christ came to do for us that which we could not do for ourselves. He developed a holy character. Not only does His righteous life cover us but, through the Holy Spirit, He imparts His character to us so that we will be in harmony with heaven when He returns.

---

[338] *Christ's Object Lessons*, p. 332.

If the heart is right, the life will be right. Covered with the righteousness of Christ, we have His character and wear the robe of His imparted righteousness, which imbues our very being with the Holy Spirit. "By the wedding garment in the parable [see Matt. 22:2–14] is represented the pure, spotless character which Christ's true followers will possess. To the church it is given 'that she should be arrayed in fine linen, clean and white,' 'not having spot, or wrinkle, or any such thing.' [Eph. 5:27.] ... The fine linen, says the Scripture, 'is the righteousness of [the] saints.' [Rev. 19:8.] ... It is the righteousness of Christ, His own unblemished character, that through faith is imparted to all who receive Him as their personal Saviour."[339] God has predestined those who have surrendered to Christ as their Savior "to be conformed to the image of His Son, that He might be the firstborn among many brethren" (Rom. 8:29).

"Christ in His humanity wrought out a perfect character, and this character He offers to impart to us" by the Holy Spirit. "When we submit ourselves to Christ," through the Holy Spirit working in our lives, "the heart is united with His heart, the will is merged in His will, the mind becomes one with His mind, the thoughts are brought into captivity to Him; we live His life. This is what it means to be clothed with the garment of His righteousness. Then as the Lord looks upon us He sees, not the fig-leaf garment, not the nakedness and deformity of sin, but His own robe of righteousness, which is perfect obedience to the law of Jehovah."[340]

Through the righteousness of Christ, both imputed and imparted, we are changed into His image and prepared for eternity with Him.

"We shall all be changed"

There are two changes brought to view in Scripture. The first is the change of our moral character. As you recognize that the Lord's "glory" is His

---

[339] *Christ's Object Lessons*, p. 310.
[340] *Christ's Object Lessons*, p. 311.

"character" (see Exod. 33:18, 19), consider Paul's words: "But we all, with unveiled face, beholding as in a mirror the glory of the Lord, are being transformed into the same image from glory to glory, just as by the Spirit of the Lord" (2 Cor. 3:18). We have already discussed this change. The second change is at the return of our Lord. The Apostle John says, "Behold what manner of love the Father has bestowed on us, that we should be called children of God! Therefore the world does not know us, because it did not know Him. Beloved, now we are children of God; and it has not yet been revealed what we shall be, but we know that when He is revealed, we shall be like Him, for we shall see Him as He is. And everyone who has this hope in Him purifies himself, just as He is pure" (1 John 3:1–3).

As Paul compared the glories of this world to the blessed hope, he exclaimed:

> But what things were gain to me, these I have counted loss for Christ. Yet indeed I also count all things loss for the excellence of the knowledge of Christ Jesus my Lord, for whom I have suffered the loss of all things, and count them as rubbish, that I may gain Christ and be found in Him, not having my own righteousness, which is from the law, but that which is through faith in Christ, the righteousness which is from God by faith; that I may know Him and the power of His resurrection, and the fellowship of His sufferings, being conformed to His death, if, by any means, I may attain to the resurrection from the dead. (Phil. 3:7–11)

And, thinking about the victory when Jesus returns, Paul wrote:

Now this I say, brethren, that flesh and blood cannot inherit the kingdom of God; nor does corruption inherit incorruption. Behold, I tell you a mystery: We shall not all sleep, but we shall all be changed—in a moment, in the twinkling of an eye, at the last trumpet. For the trumpet will sound, and the dead will be raised incorruptible, and we shall be changed. For this corruptible must put on incorruption, and this mortal must put on immortality. So when this corruptible has put on incorruption, and this mortal has put on immortality, then shall be brought to pass the saying that is written: "Death is swallowed up in victory." "O Death, where is your sting? O Hades [grave], where is your victory?" The sting of death is sin, and the strength of sin is the law. But thanks be to God, who gives us the victory through our Lord Jesus Christ (1 Cor. 15:50–57).

Chapter 15

In Eternity with Our Blessed Lord

Ever since sin entered the world, the salvation of humanity has been in the hands of Christ.[341] Now, with the redeemed safe in eternity, He sees the travail of His soul and is satisfied (Isa. 53:11). This is the joy that was set before Him which empowered Him to endure "the cross, despising the shame" (Heb. 12:2).

The love that all heaven has for us fallen human beings is beyond our comprehension. Only by the illumination of the Holy Spirit can we begin to understand God's love (Rom. 5:5), and, even still, we imperfectly understand that love, as Paul says, "the love of Christ ... passes knowledge" (Eph. 3:19). Yet, in eternity, we shall forever know that it is the love of God that redeemed us so that we may live forever with Him. We shall forever recognize that our eternal life is always and can only be because of "the righteousness of Christ imputed to us, and in that wrought," or imparted, "by His Spirit working in and through us."[342]

Our eternal inheritance

The prophet Isaiah described the coming of our Lord in glory. He wrote: "He will swallow up death forever, and the Lord GOD will wipe away tears from all faces; the rebuke of His people He will take away from all the earth; for the LORD has spoken. And it will be said in that day:

---

[341] *Review and Herald*, April 29, 1875.
[342] *Steps to Christ*, p. 63.

'Behold, this is our God; we have waited for Him, and He will save us. This is the LORD; we have waited for Him; we will be glad and rejoice in His salvation'" (Isa. 25: 8, 9). This has been the "blessed hope" from ages past. In eternity, it will be reality.

The Apostle Peter pointed his readers to our eternal inheritance reserved in heaven. It is an inheritance that will never fade away (1 Peter 1:4), for we are "joint heirs with Christ, if indeed we suffer with Him, that we may also be glorified together" (Rom. 8:17). Ellen White bids us: "Stand on the threshold of eternity and hear the gracious welcome given to those who in this life have *cooperated* with Christ.... With the angels," we cast our "crowns at the feet of the Redeemer, exclaiming, 'Worthy is the Lamb that was slain to receive power, and riches, and wisdom, and strength, and honor, and glory, and blessing.... Honor, and glory, and power, be unto Him that sitteth upon the throne, and unto the Lamb for ever and ever'" (Rev. 5:12, 13, KJV, emphasis added).[343] From the redeemed host burst forth the words, "not by works of righteousness which we have done, but according to His mercy He saved us" (Titus 3:5).

God's desire ever since the Fall has been that all of His creation experience the joy of a sinless eternity with Him. Jesus came so that we might have His joy in us. "That joy, to which Christ Himself looks forward with eager desire, is presented in His request to His Father: 'I will that they also, whom Thou hast given Me, be with Me where I am'" (John 17:24, KJV).[344] "Oh, how the divine Head longed to have His church with Him! They had fellowship with Him in His suffering and humiliation, and it is His highest joy to have them with Him to be partakers of His glory. Christ claims the privilege of having His church with Him."[345] In the judgment, Jesus has asked "for His people not only pardon and justification, full and complete, but a share in His glory and a seat upon His throne."[346] Now in heaven His divine desire is fulfilled.

---

[343] *The Voice in Speech and Song*, p. 464.
[344] *Testimonies for the Church*, vol. 6, p. 309.
[345] *Testimonies for Ministers*, p. 20.
[346] *The Great Controversy*, p. 483.

All glory to our Lord and Savior

The Apostle John saw the redeemed church of God in heaven. "And to her it was granted to be arrayed in fine linen, clean and bright, for the fine linen is the righteous acts [righteousness, KJV] of the saints" (Rev. 19:8). Although the righteousness of the saints in heaven is viewed as theirs, there is not even a thought in the mind of the saints that it was their righteousness that gained heaven for them. They all cry with one voice, "To Him who loved us and washed us from our sins in His own blood, and has made us kings and priests to His God and Father, to Him be glory and dominion forever and ever. Amen" (Rev. 1:5, 6).

"Then I, John, saw the holy city, New Jerusalem, coming down out of heaven from God, prepared as a bride adorned for her husband. And I heard a loud voice from heaven saying, 'Behold, the tabernacle of God is with men, and He will dwell with them, and they shall be His people. God Himself will be with them and be their God. And God will wipe away every tear from their eyes; there shall be no more death, nor sorrow, nor crying. There shall be no more pain, for the former things have passed away'" (Rev. 21:2–4).

Jesus said, "Blessed are the meek, for they shall inherit the earth" (Matt. 5:5). He did not mean the earth as it now is—with all its sin, war, and sickness—but the earth made new. Isaiah looked forward to this new earth when he prophesied, "the former shall not be remembered or come to mind." There shall be neither sickness, death, nor violence in all of God's new creation (Isa. 65:17–25), for "the work of righteousness will be peace, and the effect of righteousness, quietness and assurance forever" (Isa. 32:17).

In eternity, where sin will never be experienced again (Nah. 1:9), we shall sing praises to God that only the redeemed can sing. Ours will be a song of praise born of our experience of salvation through Jesus Christ our Lord and King, our Wonderful Judge.

Great and marvelous are Your works, Lord God Almighty!
Just and true are Your ways, O King of the saints! Who

shall not fear You, O Lord, and glorify Your name? For You alone are holy. (Rev. 15:3, 4)

And every creature which is in heaven, and on the earth, and under the earth, and such as are in the sea, and all that are in them, heard I saying, Blessing, and honor, and glory, and power, be unto Him that sitteth upon the throne, and unto the Lamb for ever and ever. (Rev. 5:13)

The great controversy is ended. Sin and sinners are no more. The entire universe is clean. One pulse of harmony and gladness beats through the vast creation. From Him who created all, flow life and light and gladness, throughout the realms of illimitable space. From the minutest atom to the greatest world, all things, animate and inanimate, in their unshadowed beauty and perfect joy, declare that God is love.[347]

Indeed—because our Lord and Savior has enabled us by His Holy Spirit to fully cooperate with Him in this world, we can join the apostle Paul in saying, "There is laid up for me the crown of righteousness, which the Lord, the righteous Judge, will give to me on that Day, and not to me only but also to all who have loved His appearing" (2 Tim. 4:8).

[347] *The Great Controversy*, p. 678.

Appendix

On Understanding
the Message of Scripture

1. The work of the Holy Spirit in understanding Scripture.

The first criterion for understanding the Bible is to let the Holy Spirit guide your mind in understanding what the Scriptures say. The Word of God and the Spirit of God work in harmony to guide your mind and heart in what the Bible calls "the new birth," or conversion.[348] Without the new birth, we cannot understand the truth of the Bible. For "the natural man does not receive the things of the Spirit of God, for they are foolishness to him; nor can he know them, because they are spiritually discerned" (1 Cor. 2:14). One evidence of the new birth is: "Who has the heart? With whom are our thoughts? Of whom do we love to converse? Who has our warmest affections and our best energies? If we are Christ's, our thoughts are with Him, and our sweetest thoughts are of Him. All we have and are is consecrated to Him. We long to bear His image, breathe His spirit, do His will, and please Him in all things."[349]

If you feel that you have not experienced the new birth, don't despair. Christ came into the world to give light to all (John 1:9). Moreover, God has given to everyone a measure of faith (Rom. 12:3). "But without faith it is impossible to please Him, for he who comes to God must believe that

---

[348] Jesus said, "... unless one is born again, he cannot see [*idein*—see with spiritual understanding] the kingdom of God" (John 3:3). The Apostle Peter wrote: "For you have been born again, not of perishable seed, but of [the] imperishable [seed], through the living and enduring word of God" (1 Peter 1:3, NIV).

[349] *Steps to Christ*, p. 58.

He is, and that He is a rewarder of those who diligently seek Him" (Heb. 11:6). So, exercise the faith God has given you, believe on the Lord Jesus Christ, and you will receive the Holy Spirit who will give you understanding of spiritual things (Acts 2:38, 39). Reading and believing God's holy Word produce the new birth (1 Peter 1:23).

Through Christ, God has given us the Holy Spirit to produce in our hearts an understanding of His plan of salvation. This plan, revealed in Holy Scripture, is for all who believe. It is the Holy Spirit who leads us into all truth (John 14:26; 16:13). Therefore, since all Scripture is given by inspiration of the Holy Spirit (2 Tim. 3:16; 2 Peter 1:19–21), it follows that only the Holy Spirit can give us the right understanding or interpretation of the Bible (John 16:13–15).

Our part is to pray for the enlightenment of the Holy Spirit, which only God can give. Martin Luther once said, "We cannot attain to the understanding of Scripture either by study or the intellect. Your first duty is to begin by prayer. Entreat the Lord to grant you, of His great mercy, the true understanding of His word."[350]

Ellen White summarized the process we should follow in seeking to understand the Bible: "We should exert all the powers of the mind in the study of the Scriptures and should task the understanding to comprehend, as far as mortals can, the deep things of God; yet we must not forget that the docility and submission of a child is the true spirit of the learner.... We should" study the Bible "with a prayerful dependence upon God and a sincere desire to learn His will. We must come with a humble and teachable spirit to obtain knowledge from the great I AM."[351]

2. The Bible explains itself.
The Bible is the word of God revealed to us in human language. "Holy men of God spoke as they were moved by the Holy Spirit" (2 Peter 1:21), and, if we let it, the Bible explains itself that we might know the way of salvation.

---

[350] *The Great Controversy*, p. 132.
[351] *The Great Controversy*, p. 598.

"The Bible is its own interpreter. With beautiful simplicity one portion connects itself with the truth of another portion, until the whole Bible is blended in one harmonious whole. Light flashes forth from one text to illuminate some portion of the Word that has seemed more obscure."[352] There are, however, helpful ways of examining its message. The first is by remembering the principle that Scripture is its own interpreter. Examples of this are when the New Testament interprets the Old, an incidental passage is interpreted by a systematic treatment of the subject, and a symbolic passage is understood by a passage which is fitted to teach.[353]

3. Take the Bible as it reads.

God gave the Bible so that the honest in heart may find salvation and restoration to participate in His eternal kingdom. From Genesis to Revelation, the Bible testifies to the redemption we have in Christ Jesus (John 5:39). It cannot be added to or subtracted from; it can only be illuminated. The Bible shows three eras of God's dealings with mankind for the salvation of the world: (1) the patriarchal dispensation, from Adam to the Exodus; (2) the earthly sanctuary dispensation, from the Exodus to the cross; and (3) the church/heavenly sanctuary dispensation, from the time Jesus became our High Priest in the heavenly sanctuary until He returns in glory.[354] In these eras, the priesthood took three forms: (1) the firstborn of the family was the priest, then (2) Aaron and his descendants were the priests, and now (3) Jesus in the heavenly sanctuary is our priest. Throughout these dispensations, the sacrificial lamb continued to be the central element for the forgiveness of sin and acceptance with God.

As we read, we shall see that the overall purpose of the Bible is to bring salvation to all. "The whole Bible should be given to the people just as it reads."[355] "The language of the Bible should be explained according to its obvious meaning, unless a symbol or figure is employed. Christ has

---

[352] *Our High Calling*, p. 207.
[353] *Acts of the Apostles*, p. 381.
[354] *Patriarchs and Prophets*, p. 373.
[355] *The Great Controversy*, p. 521.

given the promise: 'If any man will do His will, he shall know of the doctrine.' John 7:17."[356]

4. Let the Bible explain the symbolic passages.

There are many metaphors, or symbols, in the Bible. For example, the second coming of Christ is referred to as "a thief in the night." Because this is obviously symbolic, we need to go to an expository passage about the second coming of Christ to understand what the metaphor means. The same applies for other symbols in Scripture. Under the guidance of the Holy Spirit, we are to search the Scriptures for light and understanding of what the Word is saying (Acts 17:11).

5. One author adds insight to another on the same topic.

As God caused visions and dreams to be given to His prophets, one prophet would be impressed, under the guidance of the Holy Spirit, by certain aspects of the scene, and another prophet would be impressed by some other aspect. Yet, each prophet was writing about the same event or subject. As scripture is compared with scripture, a fuller view of the event is realized. "Bible truth ... teaches that the Christian's experience is to be one of steady growth, of constant gain in graces and virtues that will give strength to the character and fit the soul for eternal life."[357] In the same way, the revelations of God to us reveal a progression of unveiled truth from one generation to another (Isa. 58:12).

6. Use Jesus' method of explaining Scripture.

Jesus' method of giving a Bible study is instructive. He chose a topic and then showed the teaching of all Scripture concerning that topic. Immediately after the Resurrection, He chose the topic of the Messiah's suffering before entering His glory (Luke 24:13–27; 24:44). This proof-text method can be very helpful at times. It is described by Isaiah: "Whom will he teach

---

[356] *The Great Controversy*, p. 599.
[357] *In Heavenly Places*, p. 219; see also Proverbs 4:18.

knowledge? And whom will he make to understand the message? Those just weaned from milk? Those just drawn from the breasts? For precept must be upon precept, precept upon precept, Line upon line, line upon line, Here a little, there a little" (Isa. 28:9, 10).

7. Remember sanctuary imagery when reading the New Testament.
Since God's unfolding of His plan of redemption is revealed progressively (Prov. 4:18), it is very helpful to consider the sanctuary symbols and imagery of salvation in studying both the Old and the New Testaments. The church of today is now the "Israel of God" (Gal. 6:16; Eph. 2:8–16; Rom. 11:25, 26, 32). Both believing Jews and believing Gentiles are reckoned as the "Israel of God," for the New Covenant was made with the "house of Israel and the house of Judah" (Heb. 8:8–10) and Jew and Gentile are reckoned as one in Christ (Eph. 2:11–17). To be a true believing Israelite means being so in heart (Gal. 3:27–29; Rom. 2:28, 29). The writers of the New Testament were Jews who were raised with an understanding of the way of salvation as portrayed in the sanctuary. The prophecies and promises of God in the Old and New Testaments belong to those who live in this dispensation. Peter said, "For the promise is to you and to your children, and to all who are afar off, as many as the Lord our God will call" (Acts 2:39).

8. Use later inspired prophets understanding of other scriptural passages.
Four principles of understanding Old Testament prophecies are presented in the *Seventh-day Adventist Bible Commentary*. These have proved helpful.[358]

- Examine the prophecy in its entirety in context
- Consider to whom the prophecy was given and under what circumstances

---

[358] *The Seventh-day Adventist Bible Commentary*, vol. 4 (1955 ed.), pp. 36–38.

- Determine what conditions were attached to the prophecy and whether these conditions were fulfilled
- Recognize the application that the later inspired prophets made of the same prophecy; then, in this way, determine how that same prophecy is now applied.

Also helpful is to recognize that, throughout prophecy, as in the rest of Scripture, the great controversy theme between good and evil is central.

9. Remember the Spirit of Prophecy is a lesser light leading to the greater light.

"The Lord has sent His people much instruction, line upon line, precept upon precept, here a little, and there a little. Little heed is given to the Bible, and the Lord has given a lesser light to lead men and women to the greater light."[359] Of course, the greater light is the Bible; the writings of Ellen White, which God gave her for the remnant church, are a lesser light. It is vital that her writings be understood in the same way as Scripture, by comparing passage with passage. Also, as with Scripture, a statement cannot be properly interpreted if one disregards either the historical or immediate context.

10. All scriptural truth has the love of God as its foundation.

The love of God is the substance of all Scripture. God so loved His wayward creation that He gave us Jesus to be our Savior that we might be redeemed from our sinful condition. The Scriptures testify that "God is love" (1 John 4:8). Arthur W. Spalding thoughtfully wrote, "God's loving relationship to His creation [is] the foundation of all knowledge. Unless this truth [is] central in the discovery of knowledge, that knowledge [is] only a portion of truth."[360]

---

[359] *Colporteur Ministry*, p. 125; *Review and Herald*, Jan. 20, 1903.
[360] Arthur W. Spalding, *The Home Commission*, n.d., HCL6, RG104, GCAr.

Bibliography

"28 Fundamental Beliefs." Available at http://1ref.us/rq, accessed 2/27/2019.

ABSG Staff, principal contributor. "Salvation by Faith Alone: The Book of Romans," *Adult Sabbath School Bible Study Guide*, 4th Quarter 2017. Nampa, ID: Pacific Press Publishing Association, 2017.

"The Amazing Prophecies of Daniel and Revelation of Jesus Christ." *These Times*, Special Issue. Nashville, TN: Southern Publishing Association of Seventh-day Adventists, 1983.

Anthony, Catherine Parker. *Textbook of Anatomy and Physiology*. Saint Louis: The C. V. Mosby Company, 1967.

"Atonement," wiktionary, Advanced English Dictionary based on WordNet© by Princeton University, available at http://1ref.us/rp, accessed 2/27/2019.

Bauer, Walter, William F. Arndt, and Wilbur Gingrich. *A Greek-English Lexicon of the New Testament*. Chicago: University of Chicago Press, 1957.

Bowman, Robert M., Jr. "Word-Faith Movement," available at http://1ref.us/rs, accessed 2/27/2019.

Calvin, Jean. Henry Beveridge, trans. *The Institutes of The Christian Religion*, Beveridge edition. Edinburgh: Calvin Translation Society, 1863.

Canali, Fernando. Class notes "Principles and Methods of Theology," Andrews University, Winter Quarter, 1991, Feb. 21 and March 12.

Chaij, Fernando. *The Impending Drama*. Nashville, TN: Southern Publishing Association, 1979.

"Contemporary Christian music." Available at http://1ref.us/ru, accessed 2/27/2019.

Dana, Harvey Eugene, Julian Robert Mantey. *A Manual Grammar of The Greek New Testament*. New York, The Macmillan Company, 1962.

Daniells, Arthur G. *Christ Our Righteousness: A Study of the Principles of Righteousness by Faith as Set Forth in the Word of God and the Writings of the Spirit of Prophecy*. Washington, DC: Review and Herald, 1941.

Dateline: "Lutherans, Catholics, Methodists, Reformed, and Anglicans 'drawn into deeper communion.'" *Ministry*, Pacific Press Publishing Association, Nampa, ID, December 2017, p. 4.

D'Aubigne, J. H. Merle. *History of the Reformation of the Sixteenth Century*. New York: R. Carter & Bros., 1883.

"The Emmanuel Movement." *The Review and Herald*, vol. 86, nos. 9, 10, 11 (March 4, 11, 18, 1909).

Farah, Charles. "American Pentecostals: What They Believe." *Christianity Today*, Oct. 16, 1987, p. 23.

"Francisco Ribera." Available at http://1ref.us/rr, accessed 2/27/2019.

Freed, Allan. *What's All the Confusion about Tongues?* File DF311, Research Center, James White Library, Andrews University, Berrien Springs, MI.

Froom, LeRoy Edwin. *Prophetic Faith of Our Fathers*, vol. 2. Washington, DC: Review and Herald, 1948.

Goff, James R., Jr. "The Faith that Claims," *Christianity Today*, Feb. 19, 1990, p. 20.

Goldstein, Clifford. *1844 Made Simple*. Nampa, ID: Pacific Press Publishing Association, 1988.

———. "Beyond Logic," *Adventist Review*, Jan. 23, 2003, p. 28.

———. *The Great Compromise*. Nampa, ID: Pacific Press Publishing Association, 2001.

Gordon, Paul A. *The Sanctuary, 1844 and the Pioneers*. Nampa, ID: Pacific Press Publishing Association, 2000.

Gulley, Norman. *Christ is Coming!* Hagerstown, MD: Review and Herald Publishing Association, 1998

———. principal contributor. "Preparation for the End Time." *Adult Sabbath School Bible Study Guide*, 2nd Quarter 2018. Nampa, ID: Pacific Press Publishing Association, 2018.

Hamel, Paul. *Ellen White and Music*. Washington, DC: Review and Herald Publishing Association, 1976.

Harmon, Ellen G. "Letter from Sister Harmon." *The Day-Star*, March 14, 1846, pp. 7, 8.

Harper, Michael. *The Baptism of Fire*. Plainfield, NJ: Logos Books, 1970.

Hegstad, Roland R. *As the Spirit Speaks*. Washington, DC: Review and Herald Publishing Association, 1973.

"Key 73: No Violation." *Christianity Today*. Carol Stream, IL: Christianity Today International, March 16, 1973.

Kittel, Gerhard, ed. Geoffrey W. Bromiley, trans. *Theological Dictionary of the New Testament*, vol. 1. Translated and edited by Geoffrey W. Bromiley. Grand Rapids, MI: Wm. B. Eerdmans Publishing Co., 1964.

McDonnell, Kilian. *Catholic Pentecostalism: Problems in Evaluation*. Watchung, NJ: Charisma Books, 1971.

"Media on the Brain—Mini Seminar." Available at http://1ref.us/rt, accessed 2/27/2019.

Merriam-Webster Dictionary, iPad version.

Ministerial Association General Conference of Seventh-day Adventists. *Seventh-day Adventists Believe: A Biblical Exposition of Fundamental Doctrines*, second edition. Nampa, ID: Pacific Press Publishing Assoc., 1988, 2005.

Moulton, Harold Keeling. *The Analytical Greek Lexicon*. New York, Harper and Brothers, n.d.

Nichol, Francis D. *Ellen G. White and Her Critics: An Answer to the Major Charges that Critics Have Brought Against Mrs. Ellen G. White*. Takoma Park, Washington, DC: Review and Herald, 1951.

Neuffeld, Don, ed. *The Seventh-day Adventist Bible Commentary*, Washington, DC: Review and Herald Publishing Association, vol. 1, 1953; vol. 2, 1953; vol. 3, 1954; vol. 4, 1955; vol. 5, 1956; vol. 6, 1956; vol. 7, 1957.

Noll, Mark A. and Carolyn Nystrom. *Is The Reformation Over? An Evangelical Assessment of Contemporary Roman Catholicism*. Grand Rapids, MI: Baker Academic, 2005.

Palmer. "Pope Francis Sends Video Message to Kenneth Copeland – Lets Unite." Available at http://1ref.us/km, accessed 2/27/2019.

Phillips, McCandlish. "And there appeared to them tongues of fire." *Saturday Evening Post*, May 16, 1964, pp. 31–33, 39, 40.

Pomerville, Paul A. *The Third Force in Missions: A Pentecostal Contribution to Contemporary Mission Theology*. Peabody, MA: Hendrickson Publishers, 2016.

Pröbstle, Martin, principal contributor. "The Sanctuary." *Adult Sabbath School Bible Study Guide*, 4th Quarter 2013. Nampa, ID: Pacific Press Publishing Association, 2013.

———. *Where God and I Meet: The Sanctuary*. Hagerstown, MD: Review and Herald Publishing Association, 2013.

Questions on Doctrine. Washington, DC: Review and Herald Publishing Association, 1957.

Ranaghan, Kevin and Dorothy. *Catholic Pentecostals*. Paramus, NJ: Paulist Press Dues Books, 1969.

Random House Kernerman Webster's College Dictionary. New York: Random House, 1991, 1997, 2005.

The Seventh-day Adventist Hymnal. Hagerstown, MD: Review and Herald Publishing Association, 1985.

Sherrill, John L. *They Speak with Other Tongues*. New York: McGraw-Hill/ Spire, 1968.

Spalding, Arthur W. *The Home Commission*. Washington, DC: General Conference of Seventh-day Adventists, n.d. HCL6, RG104, GCAr.

Synan, Vinson. *Charismatic Bridges*. Ann Arbor, MI: Word of Life, 1974.

Wesley, John. *Sermons on Several Occasions*. vol. 1. London: Mason, 1829.

White, Ellen G. *The Acts of the Apostles*. Mountain View, CA: Pacific Press Publishing Association, 1911.

———. *The Adventist Home*. Hagerstown, MD: Review and Herald Publishing Association, 1952.

———. *Child Guidance*. Washington, DC: Review and Herald Publishing Association, 1954.

———. *Christian Education*. Battle Creek, MI: International Tract Society, 1894.

———. *Christian Experience and Teachings of Ellen G. White*. Pacific Press Publishing Association, 1922.

———. *Christ's Object Lessons*. Washington, DC: Review and Herald Publishing Association, 1900.

———. *Colporteur Ministry*. Mountain View, CA: Pacific Press Publishing Association, 1953.

———. *Conflict and Courage*. Washington, DC: Review and Herald Publishing Association, 1970.

———. *Counsels on Diet and Foods*. Washington, DC: Review and Herald Publishing Association, 1938.

———. *Counsels on Stewardship*. Washington, DC: Review and Herald Publishing Association, 1940.

———. *Counsels to Parents, Teachers, and Students*. Mountain View, CA: Pacific Press Publishing Association, 1913.

———. *Darkness before Dawn*. Nampa, ID: Pacific Press Publishing Association, 1997.

———. *The Desire of Ages*. Mountain View, CA: Pacific Press Publishing Association, 1898.

———. *Early Writings*. Washington, DC: Review and Herald Publishing Association, 1882.

———. "Words of Exhortation and Warning (Concluded)." *Educational Messenger*, Sept. 11, 1908.

———. *Evangelism*. Washington, DC: Review and Herald Publishing Association, 1946.

———. *The Faith I Live By*. Washington, DC: Review and Herald Publishing Association, 1958.

———. *God's Amazing Grace*. Washington, DC: Review and Herald Publishing Association, 1973.

———. *The Great Controversy*. Mountain View, CA: Pacific Press Publishing Association, 1911.

————. *Historical Sketches of the Foreign Missions of the Seventh-day Adventists*. Basle: Imprimerie Polyglotte, 1886.

————. *In Heavenly Places*. Washington, DC: Review and Herald Publishing Association, 1967.

————. *Last Day Events*. Boise, ID: Pacific Press Publishing Association, 1992.

————. *Loma Linda Messages*. Payson, AZ: Leaves-of-Autumn Books, 1981.

————. *Thoughts from the Mount of Blessing*. Mountain View, CA: Pacific Press Publishing Association, 1896.

————. *A New Life (Revival and Beyond)*. Payson, AZ: Leaves-of-Autumn Books, 1972.

————. *Our Father Cares*. Hagerstown, MD: Review and Herald Publishing Association, 1991.

————. *Our High Calling*. Washington, DC: Review and Herald Publishing Association, 1961.

————. *Patriarchs and Prophets*. Washington, DC: Review and Herald Publishing Association, 1890.

————. *Prophets and Kings*. Mountain View, CA: Pacific Press Publishing Association, 1917.

————. *The Review and Herald*, 1851–1959 Periodical Articles.

————. *Steps to Christ*. Oakland, CA: Pacific Press Publishing Association, 1892.

————. *Sons and Daughters of God*. Washington, DC: Review and Herald Publishing Association, 1955.

————. *Selected Messages*, book 1. Washington, DC: Review and Herald Publishing Association, 1958.

————. *The Spirit of Prophecy*. Battle Creek, MI: Seventh-day Adventist Publishing Association, Vol. 1, 1870; Vol. 2, 1877; Vol. 3, 1878; Vol. 4, 1884.

————. *Signs of the Times*, Periodical Articles, 1874–1915.

———. *Testimonies for the Church*. Mountain View, CA: Pacific Press Publishing Association, Vol. 1, 1868; Vol. 2, 1871; Vol. 3, 1875, Vol. 4, 1881; Vol. 5, 1889; Vol. 6, 1901; Vol. 7, 1902; Vol. 8, 1904; Vol. 9, 1909.

———. *Testimonies to Ministers and Gospel Workers*. Mountain View, CA: Pacific Press Publishing Association, 1923.

———. *True Revival: The Church's Greatest Need*. Hagerstown, MD, Review and Herald Publishing Association, 2010.

———. *The Voice in Speech and Song*. Boise, ID: Pacific Press Publishing Association, 1988.

White, Ellen G. and James. "To the Little Flock Scattered Abroad." April 6, 1846.

TEACH Services, Inc.
P U B L I S H I N G
www.TEACHServices.com ● (800) 367-1844

We invite you to view the complete
selection of titles we publish at:
www.TEACHServices.com

We encourage you to write us
with your thoughts about this,
or any other book we publish at:
info@TEACHServices.com

TEACH Services' titles may be purchased in
bulk quantities for educational, fund-raising,
business, or promotional use.
bulksales@TEACHServices.com

Finally, if you are interested in seeing
your own book in print, please contact us at:
publishing@TEACHServices.com
We are happy to review your manuscript at no charge.